# CliffsNotes™
# Planning Your Retirement

## By G. Michael Perry and Howard L. Sorkin

## IN THIS BOOK

- Learn the importance of looking into the future to plan your retirement

- Understand qualified retirement plans, IRAs, and Social Security

- Learn about risk management and the growth of money over time

- Get into the details of your 401(k) plan

- Reinforce what you learn with CliffsNotes Review

- Find more retirement information in CliffsNotes Resource Center and online at www.cliffsnotes.com

IDG Books Worldwide, Inc.
An International Data Group Company
Foster City, CA • Chicago, IL • Indianapolis, IN • New York, NY

## About the Author

**G. Michael Perry** has a Bachelor's degree in engineering from Northwestern University, and Juris Doctor and Master of Laws degrees from the John Marshall Law School in Chicago. He is an attorney in practice in the village of Northfield, IL. **Howard L. Sorkin** has worked in the financial marketplace for more than 20 years. A member of the Chicago Board of Trade and Chicago Stock Exchange for more than two decades, he also operates two financial consulting concerns, concentrating on advising senior citizens and those nearing retirement age on the uses of annuities and specialized insurance. He lives in Northbrook, Illinois.

## Publisher's Acknowledgments

### Editorial

Project Editor: Christine Meloy Beck
Acquisitions Editor: Karen J. Hansen
Copy Editor: Corey Dalton
Technical Editor: Bart Astor

### Production

Indexer: York Production Services, Inc.
Proofreader: York Production Services, Inc.
IDG Books Indianapolis Production Department

CliffsNotes™ Planning Your Retirement
Published by
IDG Books Worldwide, Inc.
An International Data Group Company
919 E. Hillsdale Blvd.
Suite 400
Foster City, CA 94404
www.idgbooks.com (IDG Books Worldwide Web site)
www.cliffsnotes.com (CliffsNotes Web site)

# Table of Contents

# INTRODUCTION

This book introduces you to the basics of retirement planning. Nearly everyone needs to be concerned with planning for retirement. You examine the importance of gathering and organizing information and of setting goals. You explore the legal framework surrounding the subject of retirement planning and investigate various types of investment and savings vehicles that can assist you in accumulating funds for your retirement — plans that your employer helps you with, and plans that you set up on your own. You find out important information about deferring income taxes in the process of saving for your retirement. You also take a quick look at the related subject of estate planning and learn some tips about Social Security that can help you gain a clear understanding of your own situation. By the time you finish this book, you know enough to start planning your own retirement!

## Why Do You Need This Book?

Can you answer yes to any of these questions?

- Do you need to learn about the importance of planning for your retirement fast?

- Do you not have time to read 500 pages on technical subjects such as actuarial evaluations, IRS qualification, and tax laws?

- Do you dread reading the 75 pages of legal writing that your company calls a retirement plan?

- Would you like to learn about pensions, profit sharing plans, 401(k) plans, Social Security, investing, and estate planning in a brief, easy read?

If so, then CliffsNotes *Planning Your Retirement* is for you!

## How to Use This Book

This book is set up so that you can easily find what you need. You can read the book from cover to cover or just check out the information that you need to know now and put it back on the shelf until later. Search for a particular topic in one of these ways:

- Use the index in the back of the book to find what you're looking for.

- Look for your topic in the Table of Contents in the front of the book.

- Flip through the book, looking for your topic in the headings across the top of each page.

- Look at the In This Chapter list at the beginning of each chapter.

- Look for additional information in the Resource Center, which offers Web sites and other sources that can give you more information.

- Flip through the book until you find what you want — I organized the book in a logical way.

To help you notice and keep track of some key elements in every chapter, you'll find the following three icons:

A Remember icon points out things that are too important to forget. This text is worth keeping in mind.

A Tip icon highlights words of wisdom that can save you some time and energy and perhaps spare you from a headache or two.

A Warning icon gives you a heads up on potentially dangerous situations. Skipping this information can be hazardous.

## Don't Miss Our Web Site

Keep up with the changing world of retirement planning by visiting the CliffsNotes Web site at `www.cliffsnotes.com`. Here's what you find:

■ Interactive tools that are fun and informative.

■ Links to interesting Web sites.

■ Additional resources to help you continue your learning.

At `www.cliffsnotes.com`, you can even register for a new feature called CliffsNotes Daily, which offers you newsletters on a variety of topics, delivered right to your e-mail inbox each business day.

If you haven't yet discovered the Internet and are wondering how to get online, pick up CliffsNotes *Getting On the Internet*, new from CliffsNotes. You'll learn just what you need to make your online connection quickly and easily. See you at `www.cliffsnotes.com`!

# CHAPTER 1

# UNDERSTANDING THE BASICS

- Realizing the importance of saving for retirement
- Understanding compounding of your retirement funds
- Reviewing the requirements of qualified plans
- Familiarizing yourself with retirement savings options

Everyone faces the challenge of creating — and adhering to — a solid retirement plan. Although most people don't need to become experts, you do need to understand the various aspects of a viable retirement plan.

Planning for your retirement isn't something that happens the year before retirement, just like planning for a college education isn't something you do in your senior year of high school. Both courses involve long-range plans and effort to implement the dream. Luckily, you have many tools at hand to build that retirement dream into reality.

In this chapter, you find a little about just what "retirement planning" means and about the concept of qualified retirement plans, along with a little bit of the history and the law surrounding these vehicles.

## What Is a Retirement Plan?

In the simplest sense, a *retirement plan* is your formula for determining what you want your retirement income to be and how you will finance that income. That retirement money doesn't accumulate overnight; on the contrary, you will probably have to stick to your retirement plan for most of your adult life. Working on your retirement plan is called *retirement planning.*

Your retirement plan involves at least three things:

■ **Goals:** The first step in retirement planning involves setting realistic goals for your retirement. You probably have a vision of what you want your retirement to be like, but you also need to have a reasonable expectation about the lifestyle you'll have when you retire — a practical and realistic goal of what retirement can be for you.

■ **Financial arrangements:** You need to know what your lifestyle will cost. If your vision is too rich for your budget, you may have to make adjustments.

■ **Discipline:** Knowing what the lifestyle you envision will cost, you need the discipline to save for that lifestyle over the length of your working career.

Start with the goals. Perhaps your idea of retirement is living on less money because you don't owe any debts — no mortgage or major loans. Or perhaps your dream for retirement means moving to where the cost of living is less and the money you have will go further. Or maybe you plan to implement such an aggressive retirement plan that you will have the money to live anywhere you want in a comfortable or even luxurious manner. Maybe you want to spend your time traveling from place to place in an RV, or maybe you want to do your traveling by airplane and cruise ship.

The tools at your disposal to build your retirement lifestyle include your personal savings and investment strategies and your employment-related retirement options.

- As an individual, you can save money for retirement by participating in Individual Retirement Accounts (IRAs) and other savings options ranging from certificates of deposit (CDs) and money market accounts to security investments.

- As an employee, you have the option of participating in retirement plans that meet federal regulations and, therefore, qualify participants to defer taxable events until you meet specified conditions. A *taxable event* is anything that happens concerning your finances that causes you to owe taxes.

- Even as a self-employed individual or small business owner, you can participate in various retirement programs, including the Simplified Employee Pension (SEP) program and Individual Retirement Accounts.

Many employers offer some type of retirement plan to their employees. A *qualified retirement plan* enables participating employees to save money for retirement in a retirement account that is subject to the requirements of the federal government. Money in this type of account earns *tax-deferred interest*, meaning you don't have to pay income taxes on the earnings until you withdraw the funds. However, if you withdraw money from your account before you retire (or before you reach age 59½) you have to pay your regular income tax rate on that investment, plus additional penalties.

## Why Saving Earlier Is Better

Early in your career, you may be in a low-paying job, struggling to make ends meet. Consequently, you may feel that you don't have enough "extra" income to put into a retirement plan. You may feel that you would be better off waiting until you have more money coming in — after you get that next promotion, perhaps.

But waiting isn't a good idea, for one simple reason: *compound interest*. Compound interest is what you get when you reinvest the interest you earn on your savings or investments by adding it to the principal — you earn interest on the interest you've already earned! The more money you invest in your retirement account, and the more time your savings have to earn interest, the more money you have when you retire.

Remember

Savings in your retirement account grow to far greater amounts when you start early and reinvest your interest and other earnings over time.

You may be surprised by the profound effect time has on your savings. Table 1-1 shows how an investment of $10,000 grows over time. For the purposes of this illustration, assume that the investment earns 10 percent interest per year — compounded monthly. You can see the enormous value of letting your investment grow over time. The investment doubles in seven years. In 30 years, it grows to nearly $200,000 — a 1,000 percent increase.

**Table 1-1: Growth of a $10,000 Investment with Compounded Interest**

| Years Invested | Value of Investment |
| --- | --- |
| 1 | $11,046.49 |
| 2 | $12,203.81 |
| 3 | $13,481.66 |
| 4 | $14,891.18 |
| 5 | $16,452.76 |
| 6 | $18,175.51 |
| 7 | $20,078.64 |
| 8 | $22,181.05 |
| 9 | $24,503.60 |
| 10 | $27,069.34 |

| Years Invested | Value of Investment |
|---|---|
| 15 | $44,536.55 |
| 20 | $73,274.92 |
| 25 | $120,557.49 |
| 30 | $198,350.39 |

If you're the kind of person who prefers pictures to long lists of numbers, check out the same information in Figure 1-1. The chart shows you how your money grows even faster as the years go by.

**Figure 1-1:**    Growth accelerates as time passes.

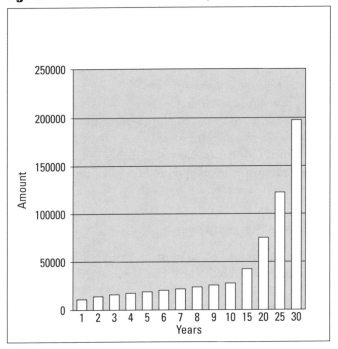

Remember

If you delay saving for retirement until a couple of years before you retire, you won't have much more than what you put in. However, if you save diligently over a long period of time (in other words, if you start your retirement plan early and stick to it), the investment returns result in a *much* larger amount than you actually invested. Begin saving as early as you can, and pay attention to your plan over the course of your career.

# Benefits of Retirement Planning

The benefits of saving for retirement seem obvious. Saving for retirement allows you to continue to live the lifestyle you have come to enjoy and expect. The good news is that qualified retirement plans also benefit employers — which makes employers more likely to offer them. Retirement plans create a win-win situation for employers and employees alike.

The most common company-offered retirement plan is the 401(k) program, covered in Chapter 5. You, as an employee, choose whether you want to participate or not. Usually, the employer offers some incentive to participate by matching your contribution with company funds. You also get to choose, within a range of options, how you want your 401(k) contribution invested.

## For you, the employee

You, the employee, benefit in many ways from your participation in qualified retirement plans such as the 401(k).

■ **Tax savings:** As an employee investing in your retirement, you receive a tax deferral on both the contribution itself for that year and on its earnings in the coming years. A *tax deferral* means you don't pay income taxes on the money you contribute to your retirement account until you withdraw that money, which may be many years later. You never pay income tax on your employer's contributions to your account.

■ **Assistance:** Without employer-sponsored qualified retirement plans, most individuals would have great difficulty setting up investment vehicles and disciplining themselves to contribute regularly to those investments. When you participate in a qualified retirement account, you receive information, in the form of monthly, quarterly, or annual reports, to help you chart your progress toward your retirement goals.

## For you, the independent planner

If you are self-employed or want a more aggressive retirement strategy than the one offered where you work, you can participate in your own retirement plan and strategies. In either case, employed or self-employed, you can participate in Individual Retirement Accounts (IRAs), which allow you to invest up to a specified amount of your pre-tax dollars in an IRA with tax-deferred benefits.

If you are self-employed, you can contribute to your own tax-deferred retirement account by participating in your Simplified Employee Pension (SEP) program. The amount of money you contribute to your SEP every year depends on the amount of money you make in the tax year. The contribution you make to your SEP is also tax-deferred until you withdraw money in your retirement years — when, presumably, you will be taxed at a lower rate than when you were earning more money.

# Qualified vs. Nonqualified Retirement Plans

Among the variety of retirement plans you can pursue, some qualify for tax deferral by the regulations of the federal government, and others don't. The federal government passed the Employee Retirement Income Security Act (ERISA) in 1974. This legislation and its requirements determine whether a retirement plan offered by employers or an employee organization (such as a union) qualifies for tax deferral of investment and interest until retirement age.

## Looking at qualified retirement plans

To qualify for tax-deferred treatment, the retirement plan must meet certain requirements, outlined in the following sections.

Qualification of retirement programs refers to standards set by ERISA and, therefore, applies only to programs offered by employers or employee organizations such as unions.

If your employer offers a pension or profit sharing plan or some other type of qualified retirement plan, your employer probably designed it to comply with all the federal requirements.

Take a look at each of these federal requirements and how the plans are designed to meet them.

- **Participation:** The plan must cover a broad group of employees, not just executives and owners. To avoid discrimination against average employees, ERISA requires that the waiting period for a new employee to become eligible in the retirement plan can't exceed one year of service or more than 1,000 hours.

- **Vesting:** Your *vesting percentage* is the amount of your retirement account balance that you own, even if you stop participating in the retirement plan today. You are *always 100 percent vested in money that you have contributed* to the plan, but you become vested in contributions made by the employer according to the *vesting schedule* set forth in the plan.

- **Nondiscrimination:** A general theme of ERISA is that a qualified plan may not discriminate in favor of executives, owners, or *highly compensated employees* (any employee who is either at least a 5 percent owner or who earned $80,000 in compensation).

If your plan is qualified with ERISA, it includes highly compensated employees and owners as well as "average" employees.

- **Funding:** Retirement contributions from both employers and employees must be kept in a trust for the exclusive use of the qualified retirement plan participants. Also, an actuary must specify how much money must go into the plan each year in order to fund the benefits it must pay in the future. (An *actuary* is a professional highly skilled in mathematical techniques for measuring risk and reward.)

- **Timing of contributions:** ERISA requires that the contributions to the retirement fund be made within specified time frames.

- **Contribution and benefit limits:** ERISA provides strict limits on both benefits and contributions the employer may make to ensure that business owners, executives, and highly paid employees don't use the plan just as a tax shelter.

- **Reporting and communication:** ERISA requires that participating employees receive a statement that explains the performance of their retirement accounts at least once a year. Most companies send out statements more often — usually quarterly or monthly.

In addition, if you are participating in a company retirement plan, you have a right to see the actual plan document and a summary plan description any time you request it from your human resources department. The plan is a highly technical, legal document that may be difficult to read and understand. The summary plan description, however, is more user-friendly and easier to read.

The summary plan description is a very valuable resource that you should study if you have questions about how your plan operates. Actually, the description is so important that you should read it even if you don't have questions about how your plan operates!

■ **Distributions from plans:** *Distributions* are withdrawals of money from the retirement plan, either at or before retirement. You can roll over the distributions from qualified plans to other plans or to IRAs. The rules governing distributions are very complicated. As you approach retirement, you may want to seek professional advice about how you should handle your distributions. Many employers offer such assistance, but you can talk with your own financial adviser to avoid confusion and tax penalties.

Distributions from retirement plans are subject to complicated tax laws and regulations that change frequently. Consult a tax or financial professional.

## Looking at other types of retirement plans

Other types of retirement plans are available to all individuals, regardless of their employment status, including the various forms of Individual Retirement Accounts, Keogh plans, and Simplified Employee Pensions (SEPs). If you are self-employed or in a very small business, your financial adviser can help you make decisions about the use of these vehicles.

In addition, many individuals take advantage of other savings plans for their retirement strategies. They may invest in certificates of deposit (CDs) or make regular investments in money markets or stocks. Some participate in investment groups and put aside a specified amount on a regular basis to invest in securities selected by the investment group.

Savings opportunities abound. The important thing is to have the discipline and commitment to your retirement to save regularly.

# Types of Qualified Retirement Plans

Retirement plans come in all shapes and sizes, but most plans fall into a few broad types. The following is a list of the major categories. I discuss the individual plans in detail later in the book.

### Defined benefit plans

A *defined benefit plan* is a retirement arrangement in which your employer guarantees the benefit. These plans usually provide a benefit related to your salary — for example, 80 percent of the average of your three highest years of compensation. Chapter 4 covers defined benefit plans.

### Defined contribution plans

A *defined contribution plan* is a retirement arrangement in which your employer contributes based on corporate performance. In other words, if the company you work for doesn't perform well one year, it isn't required to contribute to your retirement plan that year. Profit sharing plans fall into this category.

## 401(k) plans

A *401(k) plan* allows employees to contribute to the plan, on a tax-deferred basis, by authorizing their employer to reduce their salaries and contribute this reduction to the plan. Often, the employer matches a percentage of the employees' contributions. These plans have become the most popular form of qualified retirement plans.

## Other types of qualified retirement plans

Many other forms of qualified retirement plans are available, and new plans are appearing all the time. Among other plans you may know of or participate in are:

- **Section 457 plans,** which cover government employees and employees of non-religious, tax-exempt organizations.

- **Tax deferred annuities, or Section 403(b) plans,** which cover religious and charitable organizations, as well as not-for-profit organizations and educational organizations.

- **SIMPLE plans,** which are primarily for smaller employers.

- **Simplified Employee Pensions (SEPs),** which are employer-sponsored plans under which contributions are made to the employees' individual retirement accounts. The SEP plans are for very small businesses, usually those with 1 to 3 employees. In addition, the self-employed who are incorporated can participate in SEP programs.

- **Money purchase plans, cash balance plans, target benefit plans, or savings plans,** each of which is similar to a defined contribution or defined benefit plan but also has unique characteristics.

- **Keogh plans** are for self-employed individuals who are not incorporated. Any self-employed person may start a Keogh account with money earned through self-employment.

## Other Retirement Investments and Savings Programs

Most people use a three-point strategy to fund their retirement:

- **Their company-sponsored qualified retirement plan:** Those ERISA qualified plans are either the defined benefit plans described in this chapter or the defined contribution plans described in Chapters 4 and 5.

- **Social Security:** See Chapter 8.

- **Individual savings and investments:** If the company you work for offers a 401(k) program for retirement savings, the best advice is to participate fully. Chapter 5 discusses these plans. Chapters 7 and 9 cover personal savings and investing for your retirement.

# CHAPTER 2
# ASSESSING YOUR GOALS

## IN THIS CHAPTER

- Collecting your financial information
- Defining your retirement goals

Planning your retirement is part of the overall financial planning process and gives you a roadmap to reach your financial goals. Like everything in life, in order to achieve your goal, you need to identify the goal clearly and then determine strategies for achieving it.

Use this chapter to clarify your retirement goals. Take inventory of your finances to get a clear picture of your starting point — also referred to as a *financial profile*.

As the circumstances of your life change (you get married, your children go to college, you win the lottery), your financial profile does, too — and your goals may change as well. So after you create your profile, review it once a year to see whether anything has changed and then adjust your goals as necessary. The whole process is called a *periodic review*.

This chapter helps you develop realistic retirement goals based on your current financial profile and suggests financial tools you can use to convert your goals to realities.

No one can plan for retirement all alone. At various times, you may want to consult an attorney (for advice on estate planning), a tax adviser, an employee benefits specialist (perhaps from the human resources department of your employer), an investment adviser, and your insurance agent.

# Gathering Information

Many financial advisers say that you need 70 to 80 percent of your current income during your retirement years, because you expect your retirement expenses to be less than your current expenses. While some expenses do end at retirement, you also encounter new expenses, such as increased medical costs.

Many retirees find that living as a retired person costs just as much as living as a working person. In that case, you may want to postpone retirement until you save more money or be more aggressive in saving for retirement before your planned date of retirement.

In any case, your retirement goal is probably to continue living with the same or a similar lifestyle that you lead while you work. With that goal in mind, try to estimate the amount of money you need to live comfortably throughout your retirement years.

If you retire at the age of 55, your retirement package needs to be larger than if you retire at the age of 70. Life expectancy figures also influence your retirement savings.

To clarify your reasonable expectations for retirement, you need solid information. Gathering that information and staying focused and organized are important tools in achieving your retirement goals.

## Your assets and liabilities

*Assets* are the things you possess that have value because you can exchange them for cash. Your assets include real estate property you own, your personal possessions, and your financial investments. Your *liabilities*, on the other hand, are the debts you owe. Therefore, for example, the home you own is an asset, but the mortgage you owe on it is a liability. (You can find more information on how to determine your assets and liabilities, as well as their values, in the Estimating Your Net Worth worksheet.)

Assets include real estate, personal property, and financial investments. If you own business property and/or equipment, that too is considered an asset. Your real estate assets may include a home, rental property, a farm, or place of business. Personal assets include your car, your furniture, and other belongings. Some experts also list your bank account, your stocks, your cash holdings, and the interest in your retirement plan as different types of personal property, but others prefer to list these as financial assets.

Some assets are relatively simple to value — for example, a stock holding, which has a market value on any given day. Others may be more difficult — such as your grandmother's antique rocking chair or your vested retirement benefits. Usually, though, you can make a good estimate of the value of your assets based on the exchange value each has when, and if, you converted it to cash.

Obviously, some things are more easily converted to cash than others are. Converting your savings account to cash is easier than converting your car, for instance. Assets that are easy to convert to cash are *liquid* assets. Bank accounts, such as a checking or savings account or a certificate of deposit, are liquid assets.

Your *liabilities* are debts or obligations you owe and may include loans or unpaid taxes. You typically pay recurring costs, such as clothing, housing, and transportation expenses, from your current income, or *cash flow*. Money left over after paying current costs is available for you to save, invest, or pay your long-term debts.

Subtracting your assets from your expenses and liabilities gives you your *net worth*. Your net worth changes over time as your assets, expenses, and liabilities change. Like your financial profile, you must recalculate your net worth periodically. Reviewing your financial situation annually is a good tool for achieving a secure retirement.

To learn how much money you have available for your retirement years, use the following worksheet to determine your net worth.

### Estimating Your Net Worth

### ASSETS:

| **Cash and other liquid assets** | **Value** |
|---|---|
| 1.  Cash on hand | _____ |
| 2.  Amounts in savings accounts | _____ |
| 3.  Amounts in checking accounts | _____ |
| 4.  Amounts in money market accounts | _____ |
| 5.  Life insurance cash value | _____ |
| **Subtotal of cash and liquid assets** | _____ |
| **Real property** | **Value** |
| 6.  Primary residence | _____ |
| 7.  Vacation home | _____ |
| 8.  Rental property | _____ |

| | |
|---|---|
| 9. Farm property | _____ |
| 10. Other | _____ |
| **Subtotal of real property** | _____ |
| **Personal property — financial** | **Value** |
| 11. Corporate stock holdings or just Stocks | _____ |
| 12. Bonds | _____ |
| 13. Mutual funds | _____ |
| 14. Other financial investments | _____ |
| 15. CDs | _____ |
| 16. Other | _____ |
| **Subtotal of personal property — financial** | _____ |
| **Personal property — other** | **Value** |
| 16. Household contents | _____ |
| 17. Jewelry | _____ |
| 18. Collections | _____ |
| 19. Automobiles | _____ |
| 20. Other | _____ |
| **Subtotal for personal property — other** | _____ |

**TOTAL ASSETS:**

| | |
|---|---|
| Cash and liquid investments | _____ |
| Real property | _____ |
| Personal property — financial | _____ |
| Personal property — other | _____ |
| **Total Assets of All** | _____ |

Asset values can change over time, so repeat this analysis once a year or whenever a big change takes place.

## Your current income

Your income certainly affects your assets. Where does your current income come from? For many of us, it comes in the form of a paycheck. Your *gross income* is the amount you make before taxes, and your *net income* is your take-home pay.

You may have sources of income in addition to your salary, such as savings accounts, certificates of deposit (CDs) earning interest, or dividends from stock holdings. If you own rental property, the rent paid to you is income as well.

Knowing your current income and expenses is another useful tool for achieving a secure retirement. Take the time to complete the next worksheet.

Keep these worksheets and the financial information you gather about retirement in clearly labeled folders for easy retrieval. Staying organized makes retirement planning easier.

**Income and Expenses**

| Income | Amount |
|---|---|
| Net salary | _____ |
| Income from self-employment | _____ |
| Rents received | _____ |
| Child support/alimony | _____ |
| Other _____ | _____ |
| **Total of all income** | _____ |

| Expenses | Amount |
|---|---|
| Housing | _____ |
| Food | _____ |
| Clothing | _____ |
| Transportation | _____ |
| Insurance | _____ |
| Education | _____ |
| Taxes | _____ |
| Other | _____ |
| **Total of expenses** | _____ |
| **Disposable income (income minus expenses)** | _____ |

After subtracting taxes and expenses, you can use any remaining income for saving or investing.

You should earmark some of your disposable income specifically for retirement investments.

## Your retirement estimates

After you determine your current net worth and your actual income and expenses, you should figure out whether you're on target for achieving a secure retirement. If you aren't on track for the kind of retirement you want, you must either adjust your concept of retirement and the lifestyle you will be able to enjoy or take more aggressive savings and investment steps. Consider the following steps for figuring out your retirement goal and the financial requirements to make it happen.

### Estimating Your Retirement Needs

**1.** Name the amount of annual retirement income you desire. Remember that this amount is usually between 70 to 100 percent of income at retirement. _____

**2.** Name the age you want retirement to begin. _____

**3.** Find out what your Social Security benefit will be at the age of your retirement (see Chapter 8). _____

**4.** Find out the benefit you will receive from your employer's retirement plan at your retirement age.

_____

**5.** Calculate the income derived from other sources, including the sale of your home or business, personal investments, and savings.

Include all of the following that apply:

IRAs _____

Keogh accounts _____

Government benefits like veteran, disability _____

Stocks, bonds, mutual funds _____

Total _____

**6.** Calculate the total value of your assets at retirement by adding Steps 3, 4, and 5.

**7.** Estimate how long these assets will last, based on the income you identified in Step 1 and the age at which you hope to begin retirement, as identified in Step 2. _____

**8.** Estimate how much you need to save (if any) to increase your retirement funds to achieve the goals identified in Steps 1 and 2. Consider:

The number of years left to save for retirement _____

The amount of additional money you can contribute to your retirement fund _____

The estimated rate of compounded interest _____

The number of years you expect to draw retirement income. _____

## Your benefit plans

Good retirement planning also requires that you have reliable information about your retirement plans and the money in your retirement accounts. You want information on all benefit plans in which you or your spouse are participating in or have ever participated in. Get a copy of your plan's most recent monthly, quarterly, or annual report, which tells you your account balance as well as your *vesting* status (see Chapter 1 for more on vesting).

For easy access, make a folder for each benefit plan in which you and your spouse have participated. Add updated reports when you gather new information.

If you are in a qualified plan, you can get the retirement information you want by consulting the human resources department of your employer. Most of the information is contained in the plan's summary plan description. A non-qualified plan applies to an individual or a small group of key employees.

You may also be eligible for retirement benefits under some plans that have nothing to do with your employer, such as Social Security or veteran's benefits.

## Setting Goals

As you get a clearer idea of your financial profile, you can begin to identify your retirement goals.

Here are a few tips for setting realistic retirement goals:

- **Begin saving for retirement as early as possible.** For a young employee, the cost of waiting five years (from age 25 to age 30) to start investing $5,000 a year for your retirement is $408,699. That figure represents the loss of income available at retirement age due to the absence of $25,000 and its compounded interest from the retirement funds.

- **Review your retirement goals every year.**

- **Be realistic in filling out your planning worksheets.** Try to estimate your retirement expenses and determine how you can retire without debt.

- **Talk to retired people about how their expectations for retirement differ from the reality.**

- **Write a description of the lifestyle you want to enjoy during retirement.** Put that description on the refrigerator door to remind you to make aggressive contributions to your individual retirement savings plan.

- **When saving for retirement, remember the effect of time on the growth of money — compound interest.**

# CHAPTER 3
# MAKING THE MOST OF YOUR DEFINED BENEFIT PLAN

## IN THIS CHAPTER

- Understanding the concept of defined benefit plans
- Knowing what to expect
- Living with the distribution of benefits

As Chapter 1 explains, a defined benefit plan is a qualified retirement arrangement in which the employer guarantees a specific benefit for each employee. Defined benefit pension plans, generally offered by older, larger companies, cover some 40 million Americans. These plans guarantee to pay you a specified retirement benefit based on your salary, age, and length of service in the company. The longer an employee works for a company with a defined benefit program, the greater the retirement benefit.

Because the employer guarantees the benefit, it *must* contribute to the plan every year. The employer fully funds the retirement plan, and usually, the employee doesn't contribute to the plan at all. A formula that is tied to the employee's salary and years of service determines the level of the employer's contribution to the defined benefit plan.

Before the Employee Retirement Income Security Act of 1974 (ERISA), most employer-sponsored plans were defined benefit plans. ERISA's new requirements created additional administrative burdens on companies who sponsored these plans, and they responded by ending many defined benefit pension plans. Defined contribution plans, which are another retirement option, are growing in popularity. Chapter 4 discusses these plans.

## Determining Contributions and Benefits

Employers offer a fixed retirement benefit based on three characteristics:

- Salary, usually the last five years when earnings are larger
- Age at retirement
- Years of service to the company

Because of these characteristics, you can maximize the amount of your fixed benefit by delaying your retirement and, thus, adding to your years of service with the company. Sometimes staying on the job only a few more years can increase your benefit substantially — in some cases, you can even double it.

The defined benefit plan provides each participant with a specific benefit, calculated according to a formula set forth in the plan. The formula takes into consideration the following factors:

- The entire employee population
- Their vesting percentages (*vesting* is the process that entitles you to full rights to your benefits over a specified period of time; see Chapter 1)
- Their years of service
- The overall turnover rate

The professionals who manage the defined benefit funds can accurately estimate the cost of benefits at future dates. From those projected future costs and life expectancy estimates, they determine the amount of contribution the employer must make each year to fund the benefit.

The employer has to make its contribution to the defined benefit plan even if the company has done poorly and profits are down.

As with any qualified retirement plan, employees don't pay taxes on the money the employer contributes for them or on the investment returns until the employee actually withdraws the funds.

Many companies with defined benefit plans also offer 401(k) plans to employees who want to save more for their retirement by using a salary deferral arrangement. See Chapter 5 for more on 401(k) plans.

## Planning for Changes and Inflation

One of the key characteristics of the defined benefit plan is that the pension or benefit is defined, or "identifiable in advance" — it stays the same. The plan guarantees your benefit payments. The down side to that characteristic is that the plan doesn't adjust the benefit for inflation or changes in the economy.

Don't be alarmed by changes in the rules for your company's retirement plan. These changes occur often. If a change reduces benefits, the change generally applies to the years following the change and is not retroactive. Changes that occur in retirement plans generally have to do with the formula for calculating the amount of the benefit, taxation of distributions, limitations on the maximum amount of benefits, the criteria for early retirement, benefit choices, and payout options.

A person covered by a defined retirement benefit plan needs to know about the following:

- The protection of retirement funds by the Pension Benefit Guarantee Corporation (PBGC)

- The cost of living adjustments associated with Social Security

- The option of participating in additional retirement savings plans such as 401(k)s and IRAs (see Chapters 5 and 7)

## Pension Benefit Guarantee Corporation (PBGC)

The federal government insurance agency, called the Pension Benefit Guarantee Corporation (PBGC), insures the funds of defined benefit plans. The PBGC does not guarantee that the pension is as large as if the company remains solvent. If the company you worked for with a defined benefit plan goes bankrupt, the PBGC takes over benefit payments — but only to a certain limit ($36,000 a year in 1999).

Defined benefit plans are the only type of retirement program insured by PBGC.

Each year the PBGC issues a list of insured defined benefit plans that are most behind in their contributions to the pension funds they promised to their employees. Check out the PBGC Web site at www.pbgc.gov for more information. (You can find more great Web sites in the Resource Center at the back of this book.)

### Social Security adjustments

The benefit of the Social Security system that directly applies to the defined retirement plan is that the program builds in a *cost of living adjustment* (sometimes referred to as a *COLA*). Basically, the COLA means that your Social Security benefits increase to keep up with inflation, unlike your company pension.

Federal legislation determines the size and timing of the COLAs. Chapter 8 describes the Social Security system in greater detail.

## Taking Your Distributions of Benefits

Your salary, age, and years of service with your company influence your retirement benefits, but so do your marital status and decisions you make. Qualified plans protect the spouses of participants by providing two required forms of survivorship benefits:

- A pre-retirement qualified survivor annuity
- A qualified joint and survivor annuity

An *annuity* is a tax-favored investment that generates regular payments guaranteed to continue over a specified period of time, usually the participant's lifetime. A single initial deposit or series of deposits (from the company you work for, in the case of defined benefit plans) finances these regular payments. (See Chapter 6 for more information about annuities.)

### Choosing the joint and survivor option

The joint and survivor annuity requirement of a defined benefit plan means that your surviving spouse continues to receive at least half of your defined benefit after your death.

This benefit is automatic: Your spouse receives the benefit without having to do anything. In order for married participants to receive a different type of benefit, the spouse must opt out of the joint and survivor annuity. To pay for this option, you agree to take a reduced benefit at the beginning of retirement. The reduction usually runs 10 to 12 percent. The younger you and your spouse are at the time of retirement, the higher the percentage of reduction.

In some plans, your surviving spouse can choose to continue to receive 100 percent of the benefit after your death, but that option further reduces the amount of your retirement benefit. To choose this option probably means a 20 percent reduction in your monthly benefit. Even if this option is available in your defined benefit plan, you and your spouse may choose not to take this option. Your spouse does not have to make decisions about the joint and survivor annuity until you are close to retirement age.

If you know that you will probably choose the joint and survivor option, realize that doing so lowers your monthly benefits. Consequently, you probably need to save more aggressively in other aspects of your retirement plan, such as your 401(k) contributions or IRAs.

## Deciding when to take retirement benefits

Because in a defined benefit plan, the benefit relates directly to the number of years you work for a company, the longer you work there, the greater the benefit during retirement.

The cost of early retirement on your pension throughout the rest of your life is something to consider as you make a decision about when to retire. When you reach the age of 50, your company may try to lure you into early retirement by offering incentives to retire. Consider your options carefully. In a defined benefit plan, early retirement lessens the years of service and may significantly reduce the amount of your lifetime fixed pension.

If you take early retirement, you'll probably need to have an aggressive retirement savings and investment plan in operation to cover the difference between the lower fixed retirement benefit from your company and the amount of retirement income you need to maintain your lifestyle.

If you plan to take early retirement from your company with the defined benefit program and anticipate taking another job, consider this: Depending on how many years you work at the new company and how long getting vested in its system takes, the benefits of the move may not equal the benefit you would experience if you stayed with your previous company the same number of years you plan to work for the new company.

Table 3-1 demonstrates the high cost of taking early retirement for those with a defined benefit plan. This table assumes that the employee's average salary for the five years preceding retirement is $40,000 at age 55 and grows with a 5 percent pay increase each year thereafter. Actual figures for your situation change with salary changes and rates of pay increases and the formulas that determine the fixed retirement benefit. But a careful look at these typical figures suggest that if you are 60 and stay on the job for another five years, you can just about double the amount of your fixed retirement pension.

### Table 3-1:   Can You Afford Early Retirement?

| Current Age | Years of Service | Annual Pension Start, age at left | Annual Pension Start, age 65 |
|---|---|---|---|
| 55 | 20 | $7,200 | $12,000 |
| 56 | 21 | $8,467 | $13,230 |
| 57 | 22 | $9,896 | $14,553 |
| 58 | 23 | $11,502 | $15,975 |
| 59 | 24 | $13,302 | $17,503 |
| 60 | 25 | $15,315 | $19,144 |
| 61 | 26 | $17,561 | $20,906 |
| 62 | 27 | $20,060 | $22,795 |
| 63 | 28 | $22,835 | $24,821 |
| 64 | 29 | $25,913 | $26,993 |
| 65 | 30 | $29,320 | $29,320 |

## Leaving before you're fully vested

A qualified defined benefit plan may use any of several available vesting schemes, as long as it meets ERISA's requirements.

- **Cliff vesting:** The company vests employees at 100 percent after five years of employment. If you leave the company before completing five years of service, you get no benefits.

- **Graduated vesting:** The company starts vesting at 20 percent of full benefits after three years of service and adds 20 percent for each of the next four years. Vesting is complete, at 100 percent, after seven years with the company.

Any plan may have vesting that is faster than this example. These are merely the slowest speeds acceptable under ERISA.

If you leave the company fully or partially vested, all or some of your retirement benefits may be distributed to you. Most people elect to roll the distributed funds over into a special individual retirement account to maintain the tax-deferred status of these retirement funds (see Chapter 7 for more information on rollovers).

Keeping records when you change jobs is very important. The amount of benefits you receive when you leave a company may not seem like much when you leave, but remember the power of compound interest! Your records help you contact various companies or institutions where your retirement benefits reside.

# CHAPTER 4

# MAKING THE MOST OF YOUR DEFINED CONTRIBUTION PLAN

## IN THIS CHAPTER

- Understanding the concept of defined contribution plans
- Knowing what to expect
- Living with the distribution of funds

Defined contribution plans cover more American companies, large and small, than any other plan. In this type of *qualified* plan (see Chapter 1), you know the amount of the contribution made to the retirement fund — it's *defined,* or specified. What you don't know is what the value of that contribution will be when you reach your retirement age.

The size or amount of your retirement fund depends on two things:

- The amount you have contributed to the fund
- The gains your fund has made through investments

## Characteristics of Defined Contribution Plans

Defined contribution plans have several characteristics involving the following factors:

- Some plans allow you to defer a portion of your compensation and contribute it to the retirement fund, thus reducing the amount of your salary available to you.

- The employer may match some percentage of this voluntary salary deferral and contribute it to the fund on your behalf.

- Participating in a defined contribution plan reduces your current year's taxes. The government defers taxes on your contribution until you withdraw the money at retirement.

- You usually have some say in determining how you invest your contributions from a menu of investment options

- You expect the value of your contributions to increase over time, but this increase isn't guaranteed. *You* take on investment risks but hope to participate in the rewards of growing investments over time.

Some defined contribution plans allow you, the employee, to set aside a percentage of your salary, or sometimes a portion of company profits, into a retirement account. ERISA regulations and the plan document dictate the percentage that you can set aside. In most defined contribution plans, the amount that the employer contributes is discretionary and can vary depending on corporate performance or profitability.

## Determining contributions and benefits

All qualified defined contribution plans allow contributions of up to the ERISA limit of 25 percent of annual compensation for each covered employee (up to $30,000). Many types of defined contribution plans also allow employees to defer some compensation to their own accounts. In almost all defined contribution plans, vesting tends to occur faster than in defined benefit plans.

If you're seriously planning retirement, your guiding principles are these:

- The more you contribute, the greater the retirement benefit.

- The earlier you start contributing to your retirement, the more secure your retirement future will probably be.

Look at how these principles operate in Table 4-1, which demonstrates what a $2,000 annual contribution to your retirement fund can do with three different growth rates. When you reach the age of 65, your annual contribution of $2,000 (meaning that you contribute $2,000 each year) will have the following value at the indicated rate of growth. Compare the difference between starting to save for retirement at the age of 25 and starting at age 55!

**Table 4-1: Growth of a $2,000 Annual Retirement Contribution**

| Contribution Starts at Age | at 5% | at 7% | at 9% |
|---|---|---|---|
| 25 | $241,600 | $427,219 | $736,584 |
| 30 | $189,673 | $295,827 | $470,249 |
| 35 | $139,522 | $202,146 | $297,150 |
| 40 | $100,227 | $135,353 | $184,648 |
| 45 | $69,439 | $87,730 | $111,529 |
| 50 | $43,315 | $53,776 | $64,007 |
| 55 | $26,414 | $29,567 | $33,121 |

Remember

Always contribute the maximum allowed to your defined contribution plan if you possibly can.

To provide an incentive to employees to contribute to the plan, your employer may match a percentage of your contribution. For instance, your employer may add 25 cents for every dollar you contribute, or 50 cents for every dollar up to a certain percentage of your salary. In very rare cases, employers match the contribution dollar for dollar. The percent of the employer contribution represents an immediate return on your investment.

This matching contribution makes the effective growth rate of your contribution very high, just like the miracle of compound interest. Say that you make $60,000 and your employer matches 50 cents for every dollar you contribute up to 10 percent of your salary, and you contribute the full 10 percent. For the $6,000 you set aside every year, your employer contributes $3,000. If your salary remains constant, and your and your employer's contributions grow at 8 percent a year, your $30,000 investment ($6,000 every year for five years) will be worth $57,000 in five years. That represents a 90 percent gain in five years.

In salary deferral plans, the total of your contribution and your employer's match can't exceed the ERISA maximum limit, currently the lesser of 25 percent of your compensation or $30,000 per year.

Another way the employer may contribute to your retirement fund is to put a *profit-sharing plan* in place. A profit-sharing plan is a retirement plan in which the employer makes a discretionary contribution based on the amount of profit that the company makes each year. Profit sharing plans are structured so that participating employees have a stake in the performance of the company. This stake gives the employees an incentive to be more productive. Because the contribution is discretionary on the part of the employer, you have no control over the amount of the contribution.

## Tax benefits

Another great benefit of the defined contribution plan is in the tax benefit it offers you, both when contributing during the years you are working and when receiving the distribution of funds after you retire.

While you're working, the amount you contribute to the retirement plan is *pre-tax dollars* — it reduces your salary before you pay taxes on your salary. This reduction of income often reduces the amount of income tax liability in the current year. You defer paying income taxes on the amount of your contribution until the time you receive your retirement money. This is the great advantage of all qualified retirement plans.

Deferring taxes until your retirement lowers your income taxes in your retirement years, too. Because you aren't earning a salary after you retire, your retirement income is presumably less than when you were working. With less income, your income isn't taxed at as high a rate as when you were earning more. Deferring income taxes and then paying at a reduced income tax rate is considered a win-win situation for someone contributing to such a retirement plan.

## Types of defined contribution plans

The most common defined contribution plans include:

- **401(k) salary reduction programs (or the 403[b] equivalent for public institution employees):** Currently, the most popular retirement savings plan is the 401(k). Named for the section of the Internal Revenue Code that created it, the 401(k) is described more fully in Chapter 5. The vast majority of companies with more than 500 employees now offer this plan to their employees.

- **Profit sharing plans:** Contributions to profit sharing plans are at the discretion of the employer. Usually the decision whether to contribute, and the size of the contribution, are related to how well the company performed during the year. ERISA requires only that employers' contributions be "substantial and recurring." Employees may or may not have the choice to contribute to the plan itself. The biggest advantage of a profit sharing plan is that you participate in the growth and profitability of your company. If the company performs well, so do you. The downside is that if the company takes a tumble, so do you.

If your company has a profit sharing plan, ask the benefits administrator about the company's contribution to the plan over the past 10 or 20 years. This information gives you a benchmark as to what to expect from the company's contributions.

- **Employee stock ownership plans (ESOP):** Under an ESOP arrangement, a company makes shares of company stock available for your retirement account or for your purchase as a plan option. You can purchase stock without paying a commission and defer paying taxes on the value of the stock until you actually take possession of it when you retire.

Strictly speaking, an ESOP is a hybrid plan, rather than a defined contribution plan. If your company offers an ESOP and its prospects look good, it can be a great opportunity for you. Judging the prospects of these companies is often difficult, however, because most ESOPs are offered at small, privately held firms.

Your stock holdings from the ESOP may be very hard to value if the company is small and closely held or not widely traded.

- **Annuities:** See Chapter 6.

## Managing individual contributions

Many people like the fact that they have more control over their retirement investments when they participate in a defined contribution plan. Recently, more companies have begun offering employees an expanded menu of options for investing their retirement money. In addition, employees now have more opportunities to make changes in their investment choices.

In most defined contribution plans, participants have individual accounts and are relatively free to choose how they invest their contributions. Usually, the company's plan offers several investment options ranging from more conservative to more aggressive investment instruments. Typically, the choices include:

- **Mutual funds:** These funds include a professionally managed portfolio of stocks and bonds.

- **Guaranteed investment contracts**: Insurance companies that guarantee a specific rate of return issue GICs; they're similar to CDs but without federal deposit insurance.

- **Money market funds:** These funds invest in corporate or government debt; the value of shares remains constant.

- **Bond funds:** Interest-bearing securities that guarantee a specified amount of interest for a specified amount of time.

- **Employer stock:** Stock in the company you work for.

- **U.S. Treasury funds:** Lower-interest investments that guarantee the investment and the interest by the assets of the federal government.

- **Income funds:** These funds target specific types of companies for stock investment.

Historically, the best investment option has been corporate stocks. The stock market has returned an average of more than 10 percent annually since 1926. Stocks of smaller companies have done slightly better than average, returning just a little over 12 percent annually. By comparison, long-term government bonds have a total annual return of something less than 5 percent during the same period.

Despite the higher rates of returns, the U.S. Department of Labor reports that three out of four employees participating in a defined contribution plan don't invest in stocks. Research indicates that most employees tend to be very conservative in selecting investment strategies for their retirement money. Almost 47 percent of employees vest their contributions in the very conservative but guaranteed GICs when that choice is available.

## Planning for Changes and Inflation

In a defined contribution plan, you're taking a chance — a chance that change will work in your favor. Changes occur in a defined contribution plan for several reasons.

- The regulations governing the plan may change and influence the amount of your contribution, the cap to the contribution, or the size of the employer's contribution.

- You may make decisions about the size of your contribution and/or the investment options that affect the long-term outcome of the retirement fund.

- Changes in the value of the fund are related to investment trends, rates of interest, inflation, and the growth or decline of specific investment strategies over time.

For the majority of employees participating in a defined contribution plan, the most important change has been the growth in retirement funds over time. When your employer matches a percentage of your contribution, you get immediate growth in the value of your fund. Over the working years, the decisions that employees make regarding their retirement funds have traditionally resulted in growth. And historically, the rate of growth has exceeded the overall rate of inflation, which has averaged 3.1 percent annually since 1926.

## Taking Your Distributions of Benefits

Several factors govern the distribution of funds in your defined contribution plan. The following sections describe these factors.

### Vesting and leaving the company

The gradual vesting process is one way your employer encourages you to stay on the job. When you are fully vested, you "own" the rights to receive the full amount of your retirement benefit from the plan. In a defined contribution plan, this means that if you leave the company after putting in the time to become fully vested, you are entitled to all the money in your retirement account.

Your retirement account includes not only your own contributions but the matching funds your employer supplied and the investment growth resulting from the options you have selected.

All the money that *you* contribute to the benefit program is immediately your own. This portion of the retirement fund is not subject to vesting. You are always 100 percent vested in your own funds.

Even if you become fully vested in several different defined contribution plans as a result of job changes during your career, chances are that your combined retirement benefits won't equal your benefits if you had stayed put. That's because the passage of time is a powerful factor in the growth of retirement account monies.

Studies show that if you work for four different firms for five years each (a total of 20 years) and a fifth firm for ten years, the total amount of your retirement benefit will be almost *50 percent less* than if you work for one company for 30 years.

## Rollovers

When you change jobs after having contributed to a defined contributions plan, you can take the money with you, but you certainly don't want to pay taxes on this fund when you leave. The secret to avoiding paying taxes at the time you leave is to transfer the money into a special account within the time period specified by law. Such a transfer is called a *rollover*, and the most common transfer account is the *rollover IRA*, although the government also allows you to transfer the funds into your new employer's retirement plan. Your former employer must tell you how to make such a direct transfer within the 60-day period after you receive those benefit funds. (See Chapter 7 for more details on rollover IRAs.)

## Divorce

If you get divorced, your pension or retirement fund will probably be considered an asset that is subject to property division, meaning that a portion of the retirement benefit you expect to collect at retirement can be transferred to your former spouse.

## Summary plan descriptions (SPD)

Your defined contribution plan can be a complicated thing. Help is available through the summary plan description (SPD) that ERISA requires your employer to provide. Your

SPD includes information covering at least these five essential elements:

- **Vesting:** Explains the vesting procedures that apply to your benefit package

- **Retirement qualifications:** Identifies the usual retirement age requirements and how age impacts the distribution of funds

- **Benefit formula:** States the formula used to calculate benefits

- **Decisions about benefits:** Identifies the choices you have to make when retirement funds are available for distribution

- **Breaks in service:** Explains how the plan handles transfers, leaves, or termination

# CHAPTER 5

# MAKING THE MOST OF YOUR 401(K) PLAN

## IN THIS CHAPTER

- Understanding the basics
- Applying the rules
- Managing your investment

A 401(k) plan is a special type of employee benefit program that the employer sets up for the sole benefit of you, the employee. The employer acts as the sponsor, pays for the administration, and lets the employees fund their own retirements. 401(k) plans will cover more than 29 million workers by the end of 2000.

The plan is so named because you find it in the Internal Revenue Code Section 401 in paragraph k. It's the basis for all salary deferral plans such as 403(b) plans (see Chapter 6), Section 457 plans, and others. Some companies choose to call their 401(k) programs by other names, such as "our special tax-deferred savings plan" or "our savings/retirement plan." Check with your human resources personnel or manager if you are unsure whether the plan your company offers is really a 401(k) program.

If 401(k) programs were not available, many employees would have only one option for saving for their retirement — an IRA (see Chapter 7). The 401(k) plan offers you benefits that aren't available in other programs. Along with these benefits come some risks.

This chapter helps you explore your 401(k) plan and your alternatives within the plan.

# 401(k): What It Is and How It Works

A 401(k) plan is a savings plan that allows you to divert a portion of your income into a tax-sheltered savings account, which accumulates without your having to pay income taxes on it.

This program falls into the *defined contribution* retirement category (see Chapter 4) because the law defines, or limits, how much you can contribute to your 401(k) plan as a percentage of your income. The plan sponsor — your employer — must make sure your contributions comply with the law and the specific plan. In 1999, for example, the maximum amount you were allowed to defer from your income for the 401(k) plan was $10,000 or 25 percent of your pay, whichever is less, per year. (This $10,000 amount is subject to change based upon the cost of living and, of course, Congress. If Congress decides to raise this amount, the minimum increase is an additional $500 per year.)

## Employer matching

Some employers encourage you to participate in the plan by matching a part of your contributions, usually as a flat amount of, say, 25 cents for each $1 you contribute. An employer's match isn't taxable to you as current income, and the government allows earnings on this match to accumulate tax-deferred.

Knowing whether your employer matches any of your contributed funds is extremely important. Check with your human resources department, or take a look at your plan's summary plan description to find our whether, and how much, your employer matches your contributions.

If your employer matches 25 percent of your contribution (up to whatever the plan's limit is), you immediately earn 25 cents on each dollar you defer into the plan. A good strategy is to defer at least the portion of your pay that the employer matches, if you possibly can. If you don't contribute to the plan, your employer may not be required to provide any contribution for you.

Employers sometimes tie the 401(k) program to another retirement program that they sponsor, like a profit sharing plan. In this case, the rules get a bit confusing. The employer must make sure that your total contributions to *all* plans follow the maximum limits of 25 percent of your compensation or $30,000, whichever is less.

## Investment choices

In a 401(k) plan, your employer selects a number of investment vehicles from which you can choose. The employer may use a single mutual fund "family" with a choice of five or six funds or multiple fund families with as many as 50 choices. The choice of funds can range from very conservative investments, such as guaranteed interest contracts (see Chapter 4), up to more speculative and risky aggressive growth funds. Some companies let you choose which stocks you invest in, and many companies offer company stock as a choice in the program. For more information on mutual funds, see Chapter 9.

## Vesting and communication

At all times, you are 100 percent vested in the part of the contribution that is your own deferred money. That money belongs to *you*. You can take it with you when you leave that job, but you'll need to transfer it to another retirement plan or rollover IRA (see Chapter 7). Otherwise, you'll have to pay income taxes and penalties on the money, because that money was intended for your retirement.

Federal law and regulations require that over a period of no more than seven years, the contributions that your employer makes on your behalf also become 100 percent yours. This vesting schedule applies only to that part of the contribution that came from the employer's funds.

ERISA requires that the employer provide a summary plan description (SPD). The SPD describes the plan in simple, straightforward language, states all the rules, and outlines what you can do in the program. In almost all cases, your employer's human resources or payroll department lets you know what decisions you need to make, such as how much to defer, where to invest the funds, and what forms need to be filled out (and when). The remainder of this section deals with these issues.

## Getting investment education

The government requires employers to provide education to you regarding your retirement plan investment choices. This education is critical because you take charge of your own retirements in a 401(k) plan. You must be an active and well-informed participant in order to create a good retirement program. Many 401(k) plan administrators now provide self-study courses, which you can use at home or over the Internet.

Letting your money sit in money market funds or mutual funds and assuming that everything will take care of itself isn't enough — everything won't take care of itself! Your retirement depends upon your finding out what is available and getting educated.

## Evaluating investment risk

Most employers offer their employees a range of choices of funds or other investment opportunities. You must make sure that you invest your money and any matching funds from your employer to make the funds work for *your* long-term goals. You have to understand levels of risk and learn how to judge what kind of fund or investment is most appropriate for you to achieve your retirement goals.

In the world of investing, risk and return on investment generally go together.

Evaluating the amount of risk you're willing to take with your hard-earned retirement dollars isn't easy, but it is crucial. See Chapter 9 for more information on risk.

Investments are less predictable over the short run than the long run. Regular investing every payday through your 401(k) helps to neutralize short-term fluctuations in the stock market.

## Diversifying your investments

Investment advisors commonly recommend that you *diversify* your investments to spread the risk — in other words, that you don't put all your eggs in one basket. Buying only speculative, high-risk Internet stocks doesn't make a lot of sense. Neither does buying only safe, conservative investments such as government securities. Diversifying helps you to manage overall risk while producing solid returns. Mutual funds are ideal for smaller investors to use for diversification.

## Compounding

The magic of *tax-deferred compounding* is the reason that 401(k) programs work so well for so many.

■ The government immediately gives you an incentive for every dollar that you defer to your 401(k) program by not making you pay income taxes on that dollar — saving you 15 to nearly 40 cents per dollar, depending on your income tax bracket. You use *pre-tax dollars* for your 401(k). The result is that you have more dollars to invest and you lower your taxes at the same time. The higher your tax rate, the more you save. Immediately, your retirement pile of money is better off.

■ All the money withheld from your check and contributed to the plan now grows tax-deferred (meaning that you don't pay income taxes on the interest that it earns) until you withdraw it. The magic of compounding means that the money grows faster for you. You are leveraging your assets with the help of the tax collector.

Unless you participate in the 401(k) plan, your employer isn't required to contribute on your behalf. The more you defer (up to the limit allowed by law), the more investment money you get from your employer.

Table 5-1 shows an example of how $5,000 per year, set aside in your 401(k) plan, can grow over several years at various rates of return.

Table 5-1 demonstrates the magic of tax-deferred compounding. The longer the funds grow tax-deferred, the better the magic works for you, because at each level of return, the total amount of accumulated funds (plus the additional deposits) grows.

The program reinvests your previous earnings, adding to the compounded effect.

In Table 5-1, look at the 6 percent column. In 30 years, the funds grow to $395,291. Now look at the 12 percent column. In only 20 years, the funds are at $360,262. The higher the return, the faster and greater the growth.

**Table 5-1:    $5,000 a Year at Different Rates of Return**

| Number of years | 6% | 9% | 12% | 15% |
|---|---|---|---|---|
| 5 | $28,185 | $29,923 | $31,764 | $33,712 |
| 10 | $65,904 | $75,964 | $87,743 | $101,518 |
| 15 | $116,380 | $146,804 | $186,398 | $237,902 |
| 20 | $183,928 | $255,800 | $360,262 | $512,218 |
| 25 | $274,322 | $423,504 | $666,669 | $1,063,965 |
| 30 | $395,291 | $681,537 | $1,206,663 | $2,173,725 |
| 35 | $557,174 | $1,078,554 | $2,158,175 | $4,405,851 |

# Getting the Most Out of Your 401(k)

Some tips for getting the most out of your 401(k) include the following:

- **Defer as much as you can afford.**

- **Check to see whether your employer matches any deposits.** Always maximize your contribution to take advantage of this matching deposit.

- **If your income changes, double-check your program.** Make sure that your contributions are in line and that the proper taxes are being withheld.

- **Balance your investment risk by diversifying your investment program.**

- **Decide how you feel about investing.** Can you get by if you lose money? How much risk are you willing to take?

- **Define your time horizon.** How long do you have to save for your retirement?

- **Set a goal for your rate of return.** But bear in mind that the more aggressive your goals, the more likely it is that you'll have to invest in riskier investments to meet that rate goal.

- **Take risks, when appropriate.** The most conservative investment option may not always be the best.

## Investing in your company's stock

Some 401(k) plans allow employees to invest in the stock of the company as an alternative. Employees are often comfortable with this choice because they work for the company and are familiar with it. The company stock is attractive because you don't have to do any homework and you feel safe.

Putting a portion of your funds in your company's stock may make sense, but certainly not all your money. You are probably at more risk investing in your company than you realize. If your company has financial problems and you lose your job, not only are you out of a job, but your retirement plan might be at zero as well. Diversification is very important.

## Making changes to your investment plan

Be flexible. Sometimes you may want to change or rebalance your investment choices. Do it! However, just because one asset in your plan is down 15 percent does not mean, taken on its own, that you should sell it. Sometimes investors get fed up with an asset and sell it, only to find that six months later the investment recovered.

## Taking out a loan

Most 401(k) plans allow you to borrow from the plan in case of an emergency, although they usually limit the size of the loan that you can take out. Don't get into the habit of using this emergency source as an extra checking account, however. Borrowing from your 401(k) plan defeats the plan's purpose and may cause other tax problems. If you borrow from the plan, you must pay the money back within five years or the IRS considers the loan a withdrawal — subject to ordinary income tax on all the money you take out.

In addition, if you're under age 59½, the IRS assesses an additional 10 percent income tax penalty on the money you withdraw. You may also lose the right to participate in this or other retirement plans for a year or more.

Check your SPD and your human resources staff before dipping into this pot of gold. Take a loan from your 401(k) plan only after you review all your options. You must be sure that this loan gives you the best interest rate and that you can pay the money back, plus interest.

## Getting more information

As your nest egg grows into a substantial sum, you want to educate yourself and become a more sophisticated investor. Here are some ways to get more information about your 401(k) program and your investment choices:

■  See the Resource Center at the back of this book for additional books to read and for Web addresses. The Internet has detailed, understandable, current information on all aspects of investing at numerous sites.

■  The company you work for may publish a company newsletter and/or sponsor classes on investing.

■  Check your local library. Dip into good investment-oriented magazines and check out the two outstanding dailies, *The Wall Street Journal* and *Investors Business Daily.*

# CHAPTER 6

# TAX-SHELTERED ANNUITIES AND 403(B) PROGRAMS

## IN THIS CHAPTER

- Understanding the basics of annuities
- Learning about tax-sheltered annuity programs
- Understanding 403(b) programs

When you reach retirement age and receive a lump-sum distribution from your defined contribution plan, you face a tough choice. You can either take the lump sum and pay the income taxes on this probably large sum of money all at once, or you can continue to shelter the money in a tax-favored investment. The most popular choice is to roll over the money into an Individual Retirement Account (IRA). One vehicle in which an IRA can invest is an *annuity*. An annuity is a tax-deferred investment that generates a series of regular payments guaranteed to continue over the recipient's lifetime in exchange for a single payment or a series of payments. (For more information on IRAs, see Chapter 7.)

This chapter explains how annuities work and how they may fit into your planning for retirement. In addition, this chapter looks at how 403(b) programs work for employees of educational institutions and not-for-profit organizations.

## Characteristics of Tax-Sheltered Annuities

Annuities come in several varieties, but they all share the characteristics illustrated in Figure 6-1.

**Figure 6-1:**    Characteristics of tax-sheltered annuities.

 Annuities are investment vehicles issued by insurance companies and are not insured by the federal government.

 Annuities are similar to qualified retirement plans and IRAs in that they offer tax-deferred advantages to the owner.

Annuities grow in value because of the deposits you make and because the interest is both compounded and tax-deferred.

Annuities offer a steady income over the recipient's lifetime or a specified period of time (once payments begin).

The actual value of the annuity is available to the beneficiary you name at the time of your death.

Annuities can be a useful part of your retirement planning when you understand what they can do and how the different types of annuities operate.

## Fixed annuities

A *fixed annuity* guarantees that you'll earn a fixed interest rate on your deposits over the period of the contract and also guarantees a minimum payment when you begin to receive payments. As a buyer of a fixed annuity, you can choose the *term,* or period of time, you want to be locked in to a fixed interest rate. The term of the contract can vary.

The risk in selecting a longer term is that if you lock into an interest rate and rates go higher during the term of your contract, you don't benefit from the interest rate increase. On the other hand, if rates go down while you're locked into a higher interest rate with your fixed annuity, you benefit because you get the rate you contracted for. This fluctuation in the interest rate versus your locked-in rate is illustrated in Figure 6-2.

**Figure 6-2:** An example of a fixed annuity's performance over time.

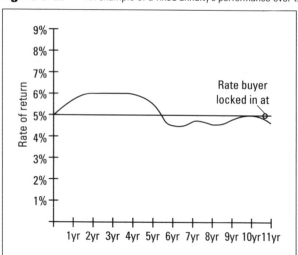

Some insurance companies provide an incentive for you to lock into a longer term when you buy a fixed annuity. These bonus incentives usually have strings attached that restrict the buyer's flexibility.

Most fixed annuities include a costly *surrender charge,* which is an additional fee you must pay if you terminate the contract early.

## Variable annuities

A *variable annuity* is a vehicle that offers a choice of investments in various *subaccounts,* or investment funds. These subaccounts act like mutual funds and you may, in turn, invest them in sophisticated mixes of various investment choices. Variable annuities guarantee a lower rate of interest than fixed annuities, but you also have the opportunity to make a higher return on your annuity investment through your choice of investments.

Variable annuities usually include an *incidental death benefit* that guarantees your beneficiary the amount of money originally put into the program plus its earnings when you die. This death benefit is very much like a traditional life insurance policy. Even if your investment choices perform poorly in your variable annuity, at the time of your death, your beneficiary receives a death benefit equal to the total premiums you paid.

The advantages of variable annuities are many:

- The chance of making money on your investments within the annuity

- Compounded interest on your principal and earnings

- The death benefit

- The tax-deferred status of this investment

However, variable annuities have disadvantages, too:

- **Fees:** The variable annuity may charge an annual contract maintenance fee, usually about $30. Each of the funds you choose to invest in may charge management fees, too. Also, you're charged fees to cover mortality and expense risk (M&E) and administration. Typically, these fees on variable annuities add up to more than the fees you'd pay on the administration of a mutual fund. The tradeoff is that annuities are *guaranteed,* while mutual funds are risky.

- **Penalties:** Although the variable annuity enjoys the tax-deferral that makes it an attractive retirement strategy, you face all of the usual government penalties for early withdrawal of funds. If you withdraw money from your variable annuity account before you reach the age of 59½, you face a 10 percent penalty on the untaxed earnings, plus the regular income taxes on these earnings. In addition, the insurance company itself may charge you a *surrender fee* to withdraw your money, which can be 9 percent or higher.

As with all your retirement investments, you stand a better chance of getting a higher return on your investment if you think long-term. You don't want to invest in a variable annuity that has great success one year and fizzles another. Look for consistent growth.

Here are five variable annuities with good investment choices and low expense fees. These offer no-load options and charge no front-end or deferred sales fees. A *no-load fund* is one that doesn't charge a fee when you open the account (a *front-end fee*). *Deferred sales fees* are charged after you open the account and it has experienced some investment returns.

■ Vanguard (800-522-5555) has seven subaccounts for its variable annuity holders. Its expenses average 0.85 percent.

■ Scudder (800-225-2470) has six subaccounts available for variable annuity investors. Its annual expenses average 1.4 percent.

■ T. Rowe Price (800-469-6587) has eight subaccount options and expenses ranging from 1.25 percent to 1.6 percent.

■ USAA (800-531-8000) has six subaccounts and charges fees from 1.7 percent to 2 percent.

■ Charles Schwab (800-838-0650) has 16 subaccounts and charges fees averaging 1.7 percent annually.

Before you buy a variable annuity, compare the answers to the questions in Figure 6-3 for at least three annuities.

**Figure 6-3:**   Requirements and conditions of variable annuities.

☐ What are the minimum investment requirements? (Usually $1,000 to $5,000.)

☐ What are the age requirements for beginning payments?

☐ What are the conditions for switching funds in the subaccounts?

☐ What are the conditions for making additional payments to the variable annuity?

## Index annuities

An *index annuity* is a relatively new type of investment that links your rate of return to the overall return of the index fund that your annuity funds are invested in. An *index fund* is one that invests in the equities that make up a certain market index. Simple examples would be a Dow Jones or S&P 500 index fund. When you buy an indexed annuity, the insurer guarantees a certain return, or *base rate,* per year. This base, or *floor,* is the lowest rate your account will earn over the period of time you choose. However, if the index fund performs well in the given year, your return is greater than the guaranteed floor rate. Index annuities offer tremendous flexibility and many options.

No one way is best for everyone, so be very sure you investigate any annuity carefully before purchasing it.

# Characteristics of 403(b) Programs

In the early 1950s, the Internal Revenue Service (IRS) established 403(b) plans to allow employees of educational institutions and not-for-profit organizations to participate in retirement plans that offered tax-deferred benefits. Originally, qualified retirement plans (see Chapter 1) excluded these employees. With 403(b) plans, these employees can contribute to a similar type of retirement program. Today, millions of Americans participate in 403(b) programs as part of their retirement planning. These 403(b) plans are sometimes called *TSAs* (tax-sheltered accounts) or simply *tax shelters* by the teachers and others who use them.

Just as with defined contribution plans, individuals participating in the 403(b) plan contribute to their own retirement account with pre-tax dollars and benefit from the tax-deferred income advantage. Federal and, often, state income taxes are deferred until the funds are withdrawn at retirement.

As with 401(k) programs, not-for-profit and educational institution employers may also make some matching contribution to the retirement fund. However, in over 90 percent of 403(b) programs, the employees are the sole contributors to the funds.

## 403(b) funds in tax sheltered annuities

Traditionally, 403(b) participants made deposits into a tax-deferred annuity program as the investment vehicle for their retirement funds. More recently, section (7) of the 403(b) program has also allowed participants to use mutual fund custodial accounts for these retirement funds. *Custodial accounts* are regular mutual funds held in qualified retirement plans.

You can put your salary contributions either into insurance company annuities (the sponsoring organization usually selects the insurance companies) or into mutual fund custodial accounts.

As with 401(k)s, the money contributed to the fund is always 100 percent your property. Your employer can't end the 403(b) plan once it's established, nor can the employer require you to transfer these funds to another account.

## Eligibility

According to 1999 regulations, you can open a 403(b) only if you work for a public education institution (including colleges and universities), a church or church-related organization, or some 501(c)(3) tax-exempt organizations such as hospitals, museums, or social service agencies. To qualify, such 501(c)(3) organizations must be a charity and not just a tax-exempt group.

## Contributions to 403(b) programs

Just as you are limited in how much you can contribute to a 401(k) program, you are limited on the amount of salary you can contribute to a 403(b) plan. Generally, you can defer up to 25 percent of your earned income, with a ceiling of $10,000 annually, whichever amount is less. Many 403(b) plans also allow you to make additional "catch up" contributions if you're nearing retirement and haven't taken full advantage of the plan in the past.

The size of the employee's contribution to the 403(b) plan has a direct impact on the amount of money available at retirement. Again, the greater the amount that you contribute, the more you have available when you retire.

## Loans from 403(b) programs

Many 403(b) programs allow participants to withdraw some of the money set aside in their retirement accounts for certain types of loans or for cases of hardship.

To avoid tax consequences when you borrow money from the 403(b) program, you need to follow the guidelines set up by both the IRS and your specific plan. The IRS has set minimum and maximum limits as to how much you can borrow — you must borrow at least $1,000, but you can't borrow more than 50 percent of the account balance, not to exceed $50,000.

The IRS further requires that you pay back the loan within five years to avoid paying federal income taxes on the amount borrowed. If you don't pay back the loan in that time, the loan is considered a distribution of funds and, therefore, is subject to federal income taxes. If you use the money borrowed from the 403(b) to buy a home, the government extends the repayment period to 15 years.

Individual 403(b) programs may vary. You should consult with your plan's administrator before withdrawing funds so that you understand the tax consequences and the repayment requirements.

## Financial hardship withdrawals

The IRS lets you withdraw funds from your 403(b) account for a *financial hardship*, defined as an immediate and heavy financial need that can't be satisfied through other means such as traditional loans.

To qualify as a hardship withdrawal, you must meet one of the following conditions:

- You're about to be evicted from your principal residence, or your principal residence is about to be foreclosed upon.

- You need the money to pay medical expenses for you, your spouse, or dependent.

- You need the money to pay for post-secondary tuition and fees.

If you make a hardship withdrawal, you can't contribute to your 403(b) plan for one year. Further, the amount of your total contribution is reduced by the amount of your withdrawal. These conditions have the effect of reducing the total value of your retirement benefit.

# Distribution of Annuity Benefits

Your investment in a tax-sheltered annuity or a 403(b) program can be distributed in a number of ways. You can transfer your funds to another 403(b) provider without adverse tax effects. You can also roll over your funds to an Individual Retirement Account (IRA) without tax consequences if you make the transfer within the IRS guidelines (see Chapter 7).

For most contributors to annuities and 403(b) plans, the time to think about distribution of funds occurs close to the time of your retirement. Several options regarding distribution are available to you, and you must make a choice that best suits your needs.

## Payout methods

One of the appeals of using an annuity is that you have basic choices about the distribution of retirement funds. If you wait until you reach the age of 59½ to withdraw your funds, you suffer no tax penalty. If you withdraw funds before that age, you pay a 10 percent penalty on the amount you withdraw.

When you reach retirement age, you can select one of many methods of payment offered by the annuity, including the following:

■ **Lump-sum distribution:** You can receive the entire amount of the annuity and either reinvest it in other retirement investments or keep the entire amount and pay your income taxes on all of it at this time of distribution.

■ **Guaranteed income for ten years:** You can receive payments that distribute the entire amount of your annuity over a ten-year period. You can usually select monthly, quarterly, or annual payments. The administrator of the annuity can tell you what your expected income would be with this arrangement. Obviously, the amount you receive relates to the size of your contributions and the rate of its growth.

■ **Guaranteed income for life:** You can elect to receive a guaranteed income for your lifetime. You can also choose to continue distribution for the lifetime of your spouse as well. Naturally, this option influences the amount of your regular retirement distributions.

## Retirement Equity Act

The distribution of retirement funds is subject to the provisions of the 1984 Retirement Equity Act. If your 403(b) is a qualified plan under ERISA, then your spouse has a right to 50 percent ownership in your retirement plan. In addition, you can designate your spouse as the beneficiary in the death benefit provision of an annuity.

You can find out whether your 403(b) is a qualified plan by checking with your Human Resources department. Most plans are not qualified.

You and your spouse should carefully consider which kind of payout option works best for you as you anticipate the retirement distribution of your 403(b) or annuity account. Many factors affect your retirement decisions, including your age and life expectancy, your spouse's age and life expectancy, and your spouse's work history.

Your retirement planning involves several instruments — your retirement plan at work is only one element. You also need to factor into your retirement equation the Social Security benefits you and your spouse expect to receive (see Chapter 8). In addition, the individual retirement investments that you have made (see Chapters 7 and 9) affect the income you have during your retirement years.

# CHAPTER 7
# IRAS

## IN THIS CHAPTER

- Understanding IRA basics
- Distinguishing between different types of IRAs
- Rolling over retirement plan distributions

Individual retirement arrangements (IRAs) come in many shapes and sizes. All of them are tax-favored vehicles designed to encourage retirement savings. Individuals can make tax-deductible contributions and accumulate tax-deferred or tax-free earnings. The IRA is a relatively new tool for retirement planning.

In this chapter, you examine various types of IRAs, their characteristics, and the procedures for making contributions and withdrawals.

The best thing you can do for yourself and your retirement years is to start and maintain an IRA.

## Types of IRAs

IRAs come in a variety of packages, including traditional individual retirement accounts — both deductible and non-deductible. Recent legislation provides for Roth IRAs and education IRAs. In addition, IRAs are commonly used to receive rollovers of qualified plan distributions.

## Tax-deductible IRAs

Deductible individual retirement accounts can't be established by just anyone; you have to have *earned income* (taxable compensation that you have received from salary or wages or from self-employment) and be less than 70½ years old. You establish an IRA with a financial institution, such as a bank or brokerage firm, and make cash contributions to the IRA each year. The contributions are *tax-favored,* meaning that they are partially deductible but not completely excluded from the income you claim on your tax return. The Tax Reform Act (1986) reduced many IRA tax benefits, including restricting the tax-deductible characteristic of IRA contributions for people with specified income levels.

With a traditional IRA, your contributions are tax-favored in two ways:

■ Part or all of your $2,000 contribution may be deducted from your *adjusted gross income* (which the IRS calls your *AGI*) for the current tax year, depending on how much you earn, so you pay less in taxes that year.

■ You don't pay taxes on the contribution or its earnings until you take the money out of the IRA.

The amount of the deduction that you can take depends on

■ Your filing status

■ The amount of income you received

■ Whether you or your spouse were covered for any part of the year by an employer retirement plan

If neither you nor your spouse were covered by an employer plan during the year, you can take a deduction for all of your IRA contributions, up to $2,000 or 100 percent of your compensation, whichever is less, unless you also contributed to a

501(c)(18) plan. If an employer plan did cover either you or your spouse, you may only be able to take a partial deduction, or no deduction at all, depending on your income. The allowable deduction becomes less as income increases.

Table 7-1 shows the relationship between income and filing status.

**Table 7-1:  How Income Affects Your IRA Deduction**

| Filing Status | Covered by Employer Plan | IRA Deduction Reduced If AGI Is . . . | IRA Deduction Eliminated If AGI Is . . . |
|---|---|---|---|
| Single, or head of household | Yes | Between $31,000 and $41,000 | $41,000 or more |
| Married, filing a joint return, or widowed | Yes | Between $51,000 and $61,000 | $61,000 or more |
| Married, filing a joint return | No | Between $150,000 and $160,000 | $160,000 or more |
| Married, filing separately | No | $ -0- and $10,000 | $10,000 |

## Non-deductible IRAs

If you don't qualify to open a deductible individual retirement account, your IRA will be non-deductible. The non-deductible IRA has the following characteristics:

■ Because your salary exceeds the established limits, your IRA contribution isn't tax-deductible. For example, if you're in the common 28 percent tax bracket, you need to make $2,778 of earned income in order to afford a $2,000 contribution, because you owe $778 in income taxes on that money.

- The $2,000 contribution you make to your IRA isn't deducted from your gross income, so there are no tax savings related to your IRA contribution.

- As long as your contributions are within IRS limits, you pay income taxes only on the investment gains, not on the contributions themselves, and these taxes on gains are deferred until you take the money out after the age of 59½.

Obviously, the tax-deductible IRA is a better deal than the non-deductible IRA is. To use a tax-deductible IRA, however, you must meet the IRA requirements.

Still, either type of IRA is a better investment than simply putting your $2,000 in an investment that taxes both contributions and earnings. To make this point, check out Table 7-2, which shows investment growth when you place $2,000 of earned income in three different retirement savings instruments — a tax-deductible IRA, a non-deductible IRA, and a non-tax-deferred investment, such as a savings account.

Both types of IRAs give you tax-deferred growth on compounded interest; but only the tax-deductible IRA gives you a tax deduction on the contribution itself. The non-tax-deferred investment has no tax deduction on the annual contribution, nor are the earnings tax-favored with a deferral until you retire. The figures show how much you would have in each account at the end of the year specified, assuming the same rates of return in each column.

**Table 7-2:   Growth Comparisons for $2,000**

| Years | Tax-Deductible IRA | Non-deductible IRA | Non-Tax-Deferred Investment |
|---|---|---|---|
| 1 | $2,000 | $1,440 | $1,440 |
| 5 | $12,210 | $8,791 | $8,314 |
| 10 | $31,875 | $22,950 | $20,085 |
| 15 | $63,545 | $45,752 | $36,748 |
| 20 | $114,550 | $82,476 | $60,339 |
| 25 | $196,694 | $141,620 | $93,736 |
| 30 | $328,988 | $236,871 | $141,018 |
| 40 | $885,185 | $637,333 | $302,717 |

## Roth IRAs

Roth IRAs became available in 1998. They differ from traditional IRAs in several ways, the most important being that you make Roth IRA contributions with *after-tax,* not pretax, dollars. That means that the earnings on the contributions and distributions are *completely free of tax.* That means that when you take the money out after age 59½, you pay no income taxes on it. In order to qualify for a Roth IRA, you must have earned income of less than $110,000 if single or $160,000 if married and filing jointly.

Roth IRAs also differ from traditional IRAs in these ways:

■ Contributions are *never* tax-deductible.

■ Distributions are income tax-free when they go to a person over 59½ who has had the Roth IRA for five or more years.

■ Income solely determines eligibility, not whether you or your spouse participates in an employer-sponsored qualified retirement plan.

■ You can contribute to the Roth IRA after age 70½.

You can take *qualified distributions* from your Roth IRA after the first five years of contributions, under one of these conditions:

■  After you turn 59½

■  For a first home purchase

■  Due to death or disability

A 10 percent penalty tax applies to early distributions from Roth IRAs, subject to the same exemptions as traditional IRAs.

## Education IRAs

An Education IRA is used to invest tax-free for a child's college educational expenses. It is *not* a retirement investment, and contributions are not tax-deductible.

## IRAs for the self-employed

Self-employed individuals and employees of small businesses can participate in a SEP-IRA (self-employed pension — individual retirement account). The SEP-IRA is a type of defined contribution plan (see Chapter 4). If you participate in another kind of defined contribution plan, your yearly total contribution can't exceed $30,000 or 25 percent of your earnings, whichever is less. If you're an employee of a small business, both the owner and you can make contributions. If you're self-employed, you can make your own contribution, but your income and filing status determines how much you can deduct on a tax-deductible basis. You are 100 percent vested in the money that either you or your employer contributes.

The biggest advantage of an SEP-IRA is that you can make larger contributions than you can with a traditional IRA.

The SIMPLE (Savings Incentive Match Plan for Employees) plans were established as part of the 1996 tax changes. They can be set up as either 401(k)s or IRAs. To be eligible for the SIMPLE IRA, employers must have fewer than 100 employees and not maintain any other retirement plan. Employees can defer up to $6,000 per year, but the actual amount is a percentage of your salary, as set in the plan document. The employer must either match the employee's contribution dollar for dollar, up to 3 percent, or make a 2 percent of salary contribution to all employees. In difficult times, an employer can choose a lower match of funds, but this option is limited to a certain number of years.

As with all IRAs, these versions for the self-employed or small businesses take advantage of the tax-deferred characteristic of the distributions and the power of compounded interest.

## IRA Distributions

IRAs are, by definition, intended for *retirement*. Therefore, if you withdraw the money early, before the age of 59½, you have to pay penalty taxes on the amount you withdraw. On the other hand, you also face penalties if you don't begin to withdraw your IRA money after you turn 70½ (except for Roth IRAs).

### Avoiding penalties before 59½

If you make an IRA withdrawal before reaching 59½, you pay a 10 percent tax penalty as well as current income taxes on the amount you withdraw. You can avoid the tax penalty if the distribution is made:

- **To the beneficiary's estate on or after your death.**

- **As a result of your disability.**

- **For certain medical expenses.**

- **If you're currently unemployed and you use it to pay health insurance premiums.**

- **To pay for qualified higher education expenses for you, your spouse, your child or grandchild:** Any college or other higher educational institution that is eligible to participate in student aid programs administered by the Department of Education is eligible for the penalty-free IRA withdrawal.

- **For a first-time home purchase:** A first-time buyer doesn't mean you have never owned a home; it means that you haven't owned a home in the past two years. The maximum amount you can withdraw from your IRA for this purpose is $10,000. Any qualified family member can use this money.

- **As part of a series of substantially equal periodic payments made over your life expectancy to accommodate early retirement plans.** You have to take substantially equal distributions for at least five years or until you reach the age of 59½, whichever is longer. The term doesn't mean that your distributions are equal payments. It means that the withdrawals are based on a set of conditions that don't change, despite the fact that important conditions like your life expectancy and the value of your IRA account change from year to year. You should consult a qualified tax professional to help you understand how these payments are calculated and the relative benefits of each method for your situation.

### Distributions between 59½ and 70½

People in the 59½ to 70½ age group have the greatest flexibility for traditional IRA distributions. You can choose to continue making tax-deferred contributions until you reach the age of 70½, and you can make withdrawals of any amount you choose. But when you reach the age of 70½, you must begin to make minimum withdrawals.

With the Roth IRA, however, you aren't required to make minimum withdrawals at any age. The Roth IRA allows continual tax-free investment growth as long you are alive, and withdrawals at any age are income tax-free.

### Distributions after 70½

With traditional IRAs, you must begin taking minimum withdrawals beginning in the year you turn 70½. These withdrawals are calculated using the life expectancy method — divide the value of your IRA by the number of years in your life expectancy. (Insurance tables and actuaries determine life expectancy figures.) Alternatively, you can determine the *joint life expectancy* for couples, which reduces the amount of your minimum withdrawals because the time line for distributions is longer. These calculations can be extremely complicated, and you need to get professional help in figuring them.

## Rollovers from Qualified Retirement Plans

Early withdrawals from qualified retirement plans are generally treated as ordinary income and taxed to the employee. In addition, an early withdrawal may be subject to a penalty tax. The best way to avoid these taxes is to transfer, or *rollover,* the assets of the qualified plan to a special IRA known as a *rollover IRA.*

The IRS taxes the rolled-over amount later on, of course, when you withdraw it at retirement. However, in the meantime, you avoid the tax, and the assets of the plan continue to accumulate earnings on a tax-deferred basis.

Rollover distributions typically occur when employees change jobs, thus ending their participation in the original employer's qualified plan. Employees have the option of leaving their funds in the original employer's plan, but many employees opt to withdraw their money. You can roll the assets over into any established IRA or establish a new one for the purpose. If you always use the same IRA to receive the rollovers, you end up with a large portion of your retirement assets in a single account. On the other hand, if you establish a new IRA to receive each rollover distribution, you may end up with lots of accounts to keep track of.

## Withholding

If any of the rollover distribution comes to you, the employer must withhold tax on the distribution. When the money is distributed to you, 20 percent is withheld, and you receive only 80 percent. If you decide to keep the distribution and not roll it over to an IRA, you owe taxes on the entire amount. You have 60 days to roll over the distribution.

## Direct rollover option

If you choose a *direct rollover option,* in which the entire proceeds are directed to a new or existing IRA, you can avoid having any portion of your distribution withheld for taxes.

The direct rollover option recognizes that because you're going to roll the distribution over anyway, you may as well simply deposit it directly into the IRA that will receive it. Because the money is never in your hands, the IRS doesn't require the withholding because you have no opportunity to do anything else with the money.

You can most easily accomplish a direct rollover by arranging to wire transfer the distribution directly to the trustee of the receiving IRA. You can also have checks sent directly to the trustee.

You must complete the rollover within 60 days of when the distribution is made, or else the distribution is subject to tax. If you choose a direct rollover, meeting this deadline is rarely a problem.

# CHAPTER 8
# SOCIAL SECURITY

## IN THIS CHAPTER

- Understanding the basic elements of Social Security
- Learning how Social Security pension benefits fit into a comprehensive retirement program
- Estimating your pension benefit
- Timing your retirement and getting your pension benefit started

Congress made The Social Security Act into law in 1935 in the midst of the worst depression of modern times. The main purpose of this law was to provide pension payments for workers and their dependents covered by the system.

Over the years, Social Security has expanded with various kinds of programs for dependents, survivors, and the self-employed. Social Security now includes a large range of other programs that have no relationship at all to retirement. This book, however, is about planning your retirement, and this chapter is specifically about how your anticipated Social Security pension benefits fit into your plans.

If you're interested in learning more about the enormous range of programs that now fall within the domain of Social Security, a good place to start is by scanning the official *Social Security Handbook,* published by the Social Security Administration. If you have access to the Internet, visit the SSA's Web site at www.ssa.gov.

## Changes Related to Pension Benefits

Over the years, Congress has legislated several important changes that directly affect the pensions of retired persons, including:

■ Large increases in the Social Security tax deducted from your paycheck

■ Raising the age at which retirees qualify for full pension benefits

The next sections discuss these changes, but the political controversies that surround them are outside the scope of this book.

In terms of retirement planning, you need to:

■ Get a clear understanding of the purpose and limits of the Social Security pension benefits

■ Maintain accurate records of your employment income

■ Estimate your future pension benefit

■ Choose the best time to start receiving your Social Security benefit

■ Know how to start your pension

## Limitations of Social Security as Retirement Income

The government did not design Social Security pension benefits to provide an adequate income for a comfortable retirement, but as a *supplement* to your income. In July of 1999, the average monthly benefit for all retired workers was $783, and for a retired couple, both of whom were eligible for benefits, the average monthly pension was $1,310. These average amounts don't provide enough income to raise you above poverty levels, and some retirees receive less than the average.

For a single retired worker, the highest benefit paid in 1999 was $1,373 a month. This maximum monthly pension is nearly double the average benefit, but by itself still provides only minimal support. Bear in mind, too, that this maximum benefit is paid only to workers who earned well above average incomes during their working years.

Social Security replaces more of a low earner's wages than of a high earner's wages. Table 8-1 compares Social Security benefits for three levels of income. (The figures are from 1997 — the latest available.)

**Table 8-1:    Social Security Benefits Comparison**

|  | Low Earner | Average Earner | High Earner |
| --- | --- | --- | --- |
| Annual Income | $12,000 | $27,000 | $65,400 |
| Percent of income replaced | 57% | 42% | 28% |

In the last quarter of 1999, the Social Security Administration began a mass mailing to 125 million workers age 25 and older who were not yet receiving Social Security benefits. The mailing consists of a four-page statement that reports each worker's previous earnings and a projection of future benefits, both retirement income and potential disability payments. If you're 25 or over, you should have received such a statement. These statements are mailed about three months before your birth month.

A key point that this mass mailing hopes to convey is that Social Security was designed to provide only part of your total retirement income. The estimate of your future monthly benefit should be a useful but sobering piece of information to incorporate into your retirement planning.

Your future Social Security monthly pension check is not a triviality, but it falls far short of what you need to maintain a middle-class standard of living after retirement.

## Paying for Your Social Security Pension

If you check your paycheck stub, you find an entry labeled FICA, which is an acronym for Federal Insurance Contributions Act. Your "contribution" is matched by your employer and is deposited in the Social Security Trust Fund. Figure 8-1 shows you how much money was paid into the Trust Fund by employers, employees, and the self-employed in 1998 (the figures used are from the IRS).

**Figure 8-1:** Comparing who pays employment taxes.

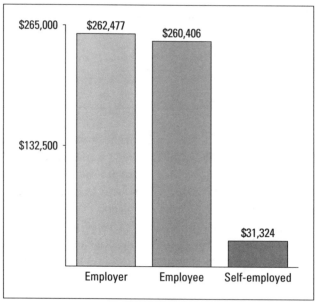

The original expectation was that the Trust Fund could fully support all future pension payments. Since 1935, several major changes have occurred both in the nation and in the program, including the increased life span of the average

American. More people are living longer, with the result that the original estimates of how much funding people would need have had to be revised sharply upwards.

To provide additional income for the Trust Fund, Congress has legislated many major changes, including:

- The worker's contribution for the pension benefit has increased from 1 percent to 6.2 percent of earned income up to a designated maximum, and the employer matches this amount. The self-employed pay both the employee and the employer contribution. The rate of 6.2 percent has remained constant since 1990.

- The "normal" retirement age of 65 is being adjusted upwards in gradual steps and will be 67 by the year 2027.

- When the program started in 1935, it subjected only the first $3,000 of income to the Social Security tax. The amount of income, called the *earnings base,* subject to the tax has risen steadily to $72,600 in 1999. The Social Security Administration calls this the *maximum taxable amount,* and it increases annually.

- Participation in the Social Security program has been extended in various ways so that coverage is almost universal.

- Cost-of-living adjustments (COLAs) were added to the benefit structure in 1972, which increased the costs of the program.

Although not part of the contribution to the Social Security Trust Fund, all employees and employers also pay, as part of the FICA, an additional 1.45 percent on all earnings (without limit on the taxable earnings base) to support the Medicare program. The total of both contributions is 7.65 percent. The employer contributes an additional 7.65 percent. So for each individual participant, a total of 15.3 percent of income, up to the base level, is contributed each year.

What does all this mean for you, the prospective retiree?

- Any significant increase in Social Security benefits is unlikely.

- You will probably continue to see raises to the contribution rate, to the taxable earnings base, and to the normal retirement age.

## Calculating Your Pension Benefit: The Shortcut

Although important changes may come regarding the Social Security pension system, right now you must live with the current realities. You can't control how much you will put into the system, you can't opt out of it, and you have only limited options with regard to the amount of your eventual pension benefit. So the best thing for you to do for your retirement planning is to figure out approximately how much your pension from Social Security is likely to be.

To request a reasonably accurate, personalized estimate of your own Social Security benefits based on your earning history, call the Social Security Administration at 1-800-772-1213 or your local Social Security office. Ask for Form 7004-SM, the Request for Earnings and Benefit Estimate Statement, like the one shown in Figure 8-2. You should get the requested information — your Personal Earnings and Benefit Estimate Statement (PEBES) — by mail about six weeks after you return the completed form. You can't obtain this information about your account either by telephone or on the Internet, although you can get the request form from the Social Security Administration Web site at www.ssa.gov. (See the Resource Center at the back of this book for more great Web sites.)

**Figure 8-2:**    The PEBES request form.

Request for Earnings and Benefit Estimate Statement

☐ Please check this box if you want to get your statement in Spanish instead of English.

Please print or type your answers. When you have completed the form, fold it and mail it to us. (If you prefer to send your request using the Internet, contact us at http://www.ssa.gov)

1. Name shown on your Social Security card:

First Name                    Middle Initial

Last Name Only

2. Your Social Security number as shown on your card:

☐☐☐-☐☐-☐☐☐☐

3. Your date of birth (Mo.-Day-Yr.)

☐☐-☐☐-☐☐☐☐

4. Other Social Security numbers you have used:

☐☐☐-☐☐-☐☐☐☐
☐☐☐-☐☐-☐☐☐☐

5. Your sex: ☐ Male   ☐ Female

Form SSA-7004-SM(Internet (9-98) Destroy prior editions

For Items 6 and 8 show only earnings covered by Social Security. Do NOT include wages from State, local or Federal Government employment that are NOT covered for Social Security or that are covered ONLY by Medicare.

6. Show your actual earnings (wages and/or net self-employment income) for last year and your estimated earnings for this year.

A. Last year's actual earnings: *(Dollars Only)*

$ ☐☐☐,☐☐☐.☐☐

B. This year's estimated earnings: *(Dollars Only)*

$ ☐☐☐,☐☐☐.☐☐

7. Show the age at which you plan to stop working.

☐☐ *(Show only one age)*

8. Below, show the average yearly amount (not your total future lifetime earnings) that you think you will earn between now and when you plan to stop working. Include performance or scheduled pay increases or bonuses, but not cost-of-living increases.

If you expect to earn significantly more or less in the future due to promotions, job changes, part-time work, or an absence from the work force, enter the amount that most closely reflects your future average yearly earnings.

If you don't expect any significant changes, show the same amount you are earning now (the amount in 6B).

Future average yearly earnings: *(Dollars Only)*

$ ☐☐☐,☐☐☐.☐☐

9. Do you want us to send the statement:
   • To you? Enter your name and mailing address.
   • To someone else (your accountant, pension plan, etc.)? Enter your name with 'c/o' and the name and address of that person or organization.

Name

Street Address (Include Apt. No., P.O. Box, or Rural Route)

City                State          Zip Code

**Notice:**
I am asking for information about my own Social Security record or the record of a person I am authorized to represent. I understand that if I deliberately request information under false pretenses, I may be guilty of a Federal crime and could be fined and/or imprisoned. I authorize you to use a contractor to send the statement of earnings and benefit estimates to the person named in item 9.

▶

Please sign your name (Do Not Print)

Date              (Area Code) Daytime Telephone No.

You should request a printout of your earnings reported to the Social Security Administration at least once every three years. The Administration is under no obligation to correct mistakes after a little more than three years.

The estimate of future benefits is based on several assumptions about your future earnings and the number of years you will be employed. As you draw closer to retirement, the estimate of future benefits becomes more accurate.

# Calculating Your Pension Benefit: Getting into Fine Details

For those interested in getting a more detailed description of all the elements that are part of the process of estimating future benefits, the best thing to do is to visit the Social Security Administration Web site at www.ssa.gov. You can download a complex piece of software called the Social

Security Benefit Estimate Program. You can also request a publication called *How Your Retirement Benefit Is Figured* or download it from the Administration's Web site.

Because your retirement financial plan, of which your Social Security benefit is one relatively small piece, is based on estimates in almost all cases, it doesn't make much sense to agonize about precise estimates of your eventual pension benefit. The following basic concepts and terms are useful to know, however.

## Coverage or full insurance

To qualify for a pension benefit, you must have earned 40 *credits* or *quarters* of coverage. Curiously, a quarter of coverage doesn't refer to a three-month calendar quarter but to an amount of earnings.

In 1999, for example, you earned one quarter of coverage (one credit) for each $740 of earnings. The maximum number of quarters of coverage you can earn in a year is four, no matter how high your earnings. The amount of earnings to qualify for a quarter of coverage can change each year. Table 8-1 details the amount of earnings you need to earn one quarter of coverage.

**Table 8-1: Earnings Needed to Earn One Quarter of Coverage**

| Year | Amount | Year | Amount | Year | Amount |
|------|--------|------|--------|------|--------|
| 1975 | $50    | 1981 | $310   | 1987 | $460   |
| 1976 | $50    | 1982 | $340   | 1988 | $470   |
| 1977 | $50    | 1983 | $370   | 1989 | $500   |
| 1978 | $250   | 1984 | $390   | 1990 | $520   |
| 1979 | $260   | 1985 | $410   | 1991 | $540   |
| 1980 | $290   | 1986 | $440   | 1992 | $570   |

| Year | Amount | Year | Amount | Year | Amount |
|------|--------|------|--------|------|--------|
| 1993 | $590 | 1996 | $640 | 1999 | $740 |
| 1994 | $620 | 1997 | $670 | 2000 | N.A.* |
| 1995 | $630 | 1998 | $700 | 2001 | N.A.* |

*Not available at time of publication

The steady upward adjustment since 1977 for earnings needed to earn one quarter of coverage reflects the upward trend in earnings nationally over the years.

To be fully covered and eligible for a Social Security pension benefit, a worker needs 40 quarters of coverage earned over a minimum of 10 years of paid working experience. Earning these quarters isn't a problem for most people because a typical work history spans 30 years or more with average earnings well above even the 1999 level of $740 a quarter, or $2,960 a year.

## Average Indexed Monthly Earnings (AIME)

How your AIME is computed is far too complicated to explain in a few pages, and not even expert financial planners need to know the fine details of the process. The AIME is a calculated average of your monthly earnings that includes an inflation-adjustment factor. In simplest terms, all your earnings for your employment career are stated in current (that is, adjusted for inflation) dollar amounts.

## Primary Insurance Amount (PIA)

After the Social Security Administration calculates your AIME, the next step is to obtain an estimate of your primary insurance amount — the amount you will receive each month if you retire at the current full retirement age of 65. This amount is less if you retire before age 65 and more if you delay retirement.

Again, the calculation of your PIA, like the AIME, is complex and too detailed for these pages. Find your PIA on the benefit statement you request from the Social Security Administration.

The government is raising the full retirement age for people born in 1938 or later. Table 8-2 shows the new schedule for full retirement.

**Table 8-2: Age to Receive Full Social Security Benefits**

| Year of Birth | Full Retirement Age |
| --- | --- |
| 1937 or earlier | 65 |
| 1938 | 65 and 2 months |
| 1939 | 65 and 4 months |
| 1940 | 65 and 6 months |
| 1941 | 65 and 8 months |
| 1942 | 65 and 10 months |
| 1943-1954 | 66 |
| 1955 | 66 and 2 months |
| 1956 | 66 and 4 months |
| 1957 | 66 and 6 months |
| 1958 | 66 and 8 months |
| 1959 | 66 and 10 months |
| 1960 and later | 67 |

## Adjustments for early and delayed retirement

If your full retirement age is 65, your pension benefit is reduced by ⅚ of 1 percent for each month you begin your benefit before age 65. Thus, for example, if you begin receiving your pension as soon as you reach age 62, your pension is 20 percent lower.

If you delay retirement after your full retirement age (currently 65), your pension benefit may be increased for the years you work up to age 70 — by as much as 8 percent per year for people born in 1943 or later. The increase is less for people born earlier.

Delaying your retirement can increase your benefit in another way. If your indexed monthly earnings are higher after reaching the full retirement age than they were earlier in your career, your monthly pension benefit is also larger. The calculations of anticipated pension benefits are very complicated. You may want to consult a financial planning expert or do your own calculation of the impact of early or delayed retirement using the Social Security Benefit Estimate Program software available at no cost from the Social Security Administration.

## Working after retirement

Working after you begin your retirement can have a negative impact on the amount of your Social Security pension if you exceed certain earning levels. The government adjusts these levels annually. In 1999, for example, if you took early retirement, you could earn up to $9,600 a year before your pension would be reduced by $1 for every $2 above that limit.

If you work after retirement at age 65, you could earn up to $15,500 in 1999 without penalty. Beyond that limit, the government would withhold $1 from your pension for each $3 of earnings above $15,500. Each year, the Social Security Administration publishes a new limit for allowable earnings after retirement before penalties take effect. After you reach 70, no penalty or reduction in pension benefits applies, no matter how much you earn.

## Beginning your benefits

When you make the decision to start your Social Security retirement benefit, you must formally apply with the Social Security system. The Social Security Administration doesn't send a blank application to you. In most circumstances, you must fill out the application at a local Social Security office or over the phone with a staff person.

You need some document that establishes your date of birth. An official birth certificate (not a photocopy) is always acceptable, but other kinds of records, such as a baptismal certificate, are also okay.

If you worked in the two years before applying for your Social Security benefits, you need to bring in copies of your wages statements (W-2s) to ensure that your official records are current. Self-employed people need to provide copies of their two or three most recent income tax filings.

The Social Security system provides meaningful benefits for survivors of retirees. Ask your local Social Security office about these benefits so that you can incorporate them into your estate plan. A competent estate planner or financial advisor will provide that information to you.

# CHAPTER 9
# RETIREMENT INVESTMENT STRATEGIES

## IN THIS CHAPTER

- Understanding the value of saving to make retirement investments
- Learning how your investments grow
- Investing for growth and safety

An essential part of your retirement planning is figuring out how to save so that you can make investments that will grow and be available when you actually retire. These savings and investments are in addition to the benefit plan(s) offered at your place of employment. Saving for retirement is also independent of your contributions to the Social Security system.

Saving for retirement begins early, not just a couple of years before the actual retirement party. The more you save and invest for your retirement, the greater the financial security in your retirement years.

This chapter emphasizes the importance of saving for retirement and explains how to look at various investment opportunities in terms of growth and stability for retirement income.

# Saving for Retirement

Spending every dollar you bring home and using plastic for whatever else you think you might want or need is easy. However, if you persist with that habit, you won't save what you need to buy a home, provide a college education for your children, or retire in comfort. If you haven't already figured out that you have to save now so that you can live the way you want for the rest of your life, consider this your wake up call.

## Setting your savings goals

Even after you recognize the need to start saving, knowing how much you can or need to set aside is difficult. A general guideline is to set aside 10 percent of your gross income. To figure out where that 10 percent can come from, review your own personal budget and learn to live on less.

For example, say that your goal is to save $1,000 a year, in addition to your contributions to your benefits plan at work. To do so, you need to put aside about $20 every week. Most people have to reduce their spending to set aside that money — it's up to you to decide where in your budget to reduce spending.

Table 9-1 indicates how an annual investment of $1,000 can grow over time.

**Table 9-1: Value of a $1,000 Annual Savings Plan**

| Year | 5% Earnings | 8% Earnings | 10% Earnings |
|------|-------------|-------------|--------------|
| 5 years | $5,802 | $6,335 | $6,716 |
| 10 years | $13,206 | $15,645 | $17,531 |
| 15 years | $22,657 | $29,324 | $34,949 |

| Year | 5% Earnings | 8% Earnings | 10% Earnings |
|---|---|---|---|
| 20 years | $34,719 | $49,422 | $63,002 |
| 25 years | $50,113 | $78,954 | $108,181 |

Set up a separate savings account at your bank and arrange to have an automatic deduction made into your savings account so that you can consider savings as a fixed expense that occurs regularly.

The goal of saving regularly is to accumulate money to make investments that earn a significant return and, with compounded interest, help provide for a comfortable retirement.

## How investments grow

The savings you collect grow over time when you invest them in vehicles that have a realistic expectation for long-term growth. Over time, with a 10 to 12 percent return compounded annually, your retirement investments can become a solid foundation for a comfortable retirement.

To figure out how long your retirement investments will take to double in value, use what is popularly called the *Rule of 72*. The Rule of 72 states that, at a 1 percent return, an investment doubles in approximately 72 years. Therefore, if you earn 10 percent, your investment would double in 7.2 years. Table 9-2 shows you the Rule of 72 at different rates of return.

**Table 9-2:   The Rule of 72**

| Rate of Return | 1% | 2% | 3% | 4% | 5% | 6% | 7% | 8% | 9% | 10% |
|---|---|---|---|---|---|---|---|---|---|---|
| Years to Double | 72 | 36 | 24 | 18 | 14 | 12 | 10 | 9 | 8 | 7.2 |

Remember

The Rule of 72 helps you estimate how long your retirement savings will take to double in value. Your goal is to make your investments double in value at a faster rate. The speed with which your investment doubles depends on the overall rate of return you receive on your investments.

## Learning the investment lingo

Before you consider what to do with the retirement money you save, you need to know the language of investments. In addition to the terms used in this book, you will encounter these terms:

- **Blue chip:** Stock issued by a well-known, respected company with a record of good earnings and dividend payments.

- **Capital gain or loss:** The profit or loss resulting from the sale of investments.

- **Dividend reinvestment plan:** Also called a DRP or DRIP, this plan allows the company to reinvest a shareholder's dividends in additional shares, often at no brokerage charge. DRPs are a form of compound interest and help create additional value.

- **Dollar cost averaging:** A strategy for investing a set amount of money on a regular basis, regardless of the share price at the time.

- **Liquidity:** The ability to convert an investment into cash quickly without taking a loss in value.

- **Money market funds:** A mutual fund that invests in short-term debts and passes the interest on to shareholders. The share value doesn't change and has a high degree of liquidity.

■ **Mutual funds:** A professionally managed pool of stocks and bonds with shares sold to investors. Minimum purchases (often $500) are often required.

■ **Real estate investment trust (REIT):** An investment company that buys real estate properties or mortgages and passes the profits on to the shareholders.

# Considering Your Risk Tolerance

Before you invest your hard-earned savings, consider that all investments carry some risk. Some investments, like junk bonds or commodity trading, involve high risk. Investors who are very averse to risk tend to put their money in very safe investments that offer a predictable and reliable rate of return. Such investments include insured savings accounts, certificates of deposit (CDs), and U.S. government securities. The rate of return on these kinds of investments can run as high as two to four percentage points above the current rate of inflation, but the value of your investment actually decreases during a time of interest rate increases. In some senses, then, these investments are safe, but they are not very profitable, and they are risky under certain conditions.

The stocks of large, mature companies such as IBM, AT&T, GE, and Dow Chemical often return profits of 10 to 15 percent over the years but are somewhat riskier. Among even riskier stocks today are those of new and emerging high-tech companies, especially those relating to computers and the Internet. Some of these stocks have doubled and tripled in a few years. You have probably heard stories about people who invested $10,000 in Microsoft in the mid-1980s and have seen their original investment increase to over a $1 million. On the other hand, you have probably heard very little about "hot" stocks that failed miserably. Nevertheless, a lot of them do.

## Determining your risk profile

Investing is a delicate balance of risk and return. Your risk profile is based on your psychological makeup, your financial wherewithal, and your age. If you're very fearful of any loss, you would be wise to avoid investing in either companies or investment types that you do not understand. If you're a risk-taker, you may be inclined to put a large part of your investment money into aggressive growth stocks.

Your willingness to assume risk also relates to your time horizon. If you're going to need your invested money in a few years — for your child's education, perhaps — you may be inclined to invest more conservatively to avoid losses if the value of your stock market investment goes down when you need the money.

If all this talk of risk and return seems terribly complicated, be aware that most of the time your investment choices are limited to a relatively small number of mutual funds. Federal securities laws require that all of these funds issue a document called a *prospectus,* which tells you what type of fund it is (preservation of capital, conservative, balance of growth and income, aggressive growth, and so on), and what stocks and other investments it holds.

Follow the advice of Peter Lynch and Warren Buffett, two of the most successful and best-known money managers in the world, and *do not invest in anything you don't understand.* Before you invest, make sure you know the kind of investment you're making and the amount of risk that it carries.

## Distributing your risk

Your goal is to distribute your investments so that you balance low and high risk factors. Use the "pyramid of risk," shown in Figure 9-1, to guide your distribution of risk. At the base are relatively low-risk investments — where you probably want most of your investment money to go. At the top of the pyramid are the higher-risk ventures, which should represent just a fraction of your entire investment strategy.

**Figure 9-1:**  The pyramid of risk.

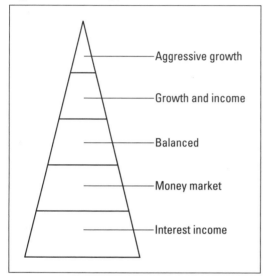

## Stock market movement

Investors should try to *maximize* return and *minimize* risk. The first question to consider is "What is your time horizon?" or "How many years do you have until you need the money for retirement?" If retirement stays at age 65, you can invest your money for maybe 40 years if you're 25 now. If you're 45, you have about 20 years, and, of course, if you're 55, you have about ten years.

During that time, the stock market will probably experience ups and downs and periods where prices seem to move sideways within a narrow trading range. Over the past 50 years, the average rate of return for stocks has been 10.7 percent. During the 1990s, the rate has been much higher, averaging a higher rate of return than ever before in history. In 1998, stock market gains, as measured by the S&P 500 Index, showed a net increase of approximately 28 percent by the end of the year, even though the Index had declined early in the year. However, in some years (about 34 percent of the time), this index averaged less than 7 percent, and in some years the market lost money.

The longer the time horizon until you need the money, the less impact one bad day, week, month, year, or bear market has on your savings because you have plenty of time to recover. If you need $15,000 for college in September, however, you may be dismayed if the market takes a downturn in August.

# Maximizing the Money You Save for Retirement

When you begin a savings plan for retirement, you need to make decisions about how to invest the money you save, based on your retirement goals, the length of time you have to achieve them, and the amount of money you can set aside.

## Dollar cost averaging investments

Dollar cost averaging is a reliable way to make regular investments. You invest a fixed amount — whatever your budget allows — on a monthly basis. Over the long term, with dollar cost averaging, you can buy more shares at a lower price because the market is rising overall.

## Reducing brokerage commissions

You may feel more comfortable using the services of a brokerage firm for transactions, in order to benefit from the knowledge and expertise of a broker. However, if you want to minimize brokerage fees and are willing to take on the task of researching investments yourself, you can reduce the brokerage commissions you pay through the following methods:

- **Buy direct:** Some companies are willing to sell shares directly to investors. Many also allow the investor to participate in the company's dividend reinvestment plan (DRIP).

    To check for companies that allow for direct investments, contact:

    *The Moneypaper* at 1-800-388-9993 or www.moneypaper.com.

    *Netstock Direct* at 1-888-638-7865 or www.netstockdirect.com.

- **Pursue no-load mutual funds:** A *no-load* fund is one that doesn't add charges, either when you buy (called a *front-end* sales commission) or when you sell (called a *back-end* fee). You can invest a small or large amount of money on a regular basis even if your investment dollars only buy fractional shares. Many of these no-load mutual funds work with automatic deductions from your bank account.

### Using qualified financial planners

You may want to work with a professional financial planner who can help you analyze your retirement goals and strategies and recommend the balance in your investment *portfolio,* or collection of investments, that works best for you.

Financial planners are trained professionals. Get recommendations from your accountant or tax preparer or by consulting a directory of these professionals in your area. Certified financial planners (CFPs) have taken a series of courses, passed a six-part exam, and have a minimum of three years of experience.

You can get the names of CFPs in your area from:

- The International Association for Financial Planning at 5755 Glenridge Drive NE, Suite B300, Atlanta, GA 30328; phone 1-800-945-4237.

- The Institute of Certified Financial Planners at 3801 E. Florida Avenue, Suite 708, Denver, CO 80210; phone 1-303-759-4900.

There are no set fees for financial planners; some work for a fee, others work on commissions, and some are paid with a combination of the two methods.

If you decide to use a financial planner, interview at least three candidates and ask each about their fees and their experience. Ask also to see their resumes and a list of references.

## The benefits of mutual funds

In the long run, the performance of mutual funds has been strong, generating respectable rates of return for investors. In addition, they give the small investor the benefit of access to professional money managers who analyze the reports of thousands of companies in order to compile a suitable portfolio.

A mutual fund is a company that pools the money of many investors and buys a collection of investment vehicles intended to achieve a specific goal. Mutual funds are a great way for novice investors, who worry about their own ability to select stocks, to make informed choices. Most mutual funds specialize in certain types of stocks and bonds. For example, some funds may concentrate on investing in international companies specializing in technology development. Other funds specialize in utility companies, or focus on growth, small companies, or government bonds.

Compare the performance of the following types of mutual funds over a long period of time. Many have an annual return of over 10 percent. The figures in Table 9-3 show the average annual return since the date indicated to 1995.

**Table 9-3: Performance of Selected Types of Mutual Funds**

| Type of Fund | 1970 | 1980 | 1990 |
|---|---|---|---|
| Global | 13.4% | 15.2% | 6.1% |
| Growth & income | 10.6% | 13.2% | 8.2% |
| Science & technology | 9.4% | 12.3% | 16.7% |
| Government bonds | 9.3% | 9.5% | 6.5% |
| Utilities | 8.7% | 11.0% | 6.5% |

Thousands of mutual funds are available. After you determine the amount of risk you want to carry with your investment, you can sort out the mutual funds that meet your requirements. To get reliable information about mutual funds, you can consult the business section of your local newspaper or the business papers and magazines that are commonly available. If you choose to work with a financial planner, this professional can help guide your choices.

## Retirement investment tips

Your retirement will be more comfortable and worry-free when you take advantage of the following strategies:

- **Contribute to your retirement plan at work to the maximum degree possible:** Take advantage of all matching funds your employer will put in your 401(k).

- **Keep up with the changes and trends in Social Security:** Know how your Social Security benefit fits into your retirement plans.

- **Save and invest regularly for your own retirement:** Small but regular savings are easier on your budget than large lump sums.

- **Start now:** Retirement may seem like a lifetime away when you're in your 20s, when getting a good job and buying a home seem to be your top priorities. However, all the data show that when you start saving for retirement early on, your savings and investments can provide a comfortable retirement and financial security that you can't achieve when you start later. Remember the miracle of compound interest.

- **Diversify your investments:** Don't put your retirement nest egg into one basket. Investing in a mutual fund provides some kind of diversity. Include a variable annuity, additional mutual funds, a Roth IRA, or other instruments in your retirement portfolio.

- **Do something:** No decision is foolproof, but take that first step anyway. If you aren't happy with the results over a period of time, don't be afraid to make a change.

# CHAPTER 10

# ESTATE PLANNING

## IN THIS CHAPTER

- Understanding estate planning
- Taking a look at estate and inheritance taxes
- Knowing what goes into a will
- Making an inventory of your assets

The assets that you accumulate during your lifetime go to your heirs upon your death. The possibilities for trouble are endless, and so is the range of possible solutions. This chapter looks at some of the basic documents you need for your estate planning.

## Exploring the Basics of Estate Planning

*Estate planning* refers to the process of putting your affairs in order so that, upon your death, you pass on as much of your assets (or *estate*) as possible to your designated *beneficiaries* or *heirs* in an orderly transition. Your beneficiaries receive the proceeds of your estate by your direction made in writing. Your heirs, on the other hand, are relatives who receive your assets as a matter of law if you don't specify otherwise.

The basic goal of estate planning is to make sure that your estate passes to those whom you want to receive it, at the least possible cost in taxes and administrative expenses.

# Estate and Inheritance Taxes

The government may confiscate a portion of your estate through death taxes. The federal government refers to its death tax as the *estate tax,* and state governments call their death taxes *inheritance taxes.*

The federal estate tax applies to property that you transfer to another at your death. The tax is on the *transfer* of the property and is proportional to the overall value of the estate. In this sense, the tax may also apply to other transfers of property, such as gifts made before death. Under the federal system, the government may subject money or property you give to someone before your death to the estate tax — the *estate and gift tax.*

Fortunately, the estate tax only applies to the value of your estate that is above the *applicable exclusion amount.* That amount changes year to year, as shown in Figure 10-1. This exemption means that you can transfer up to the given amount for that year in property totally free of estate taxes. The estate and gift tax on any amount exceeding the applicable exclusion amount may be 55 percent or higher.

**Figure 10-1:** The applicable exclusion amounts.

| Year | Applicable Exclusion Amount |
|------|------------------------------|
| 1999 | $650,000 |
| 2000 | $675,000 |
| 2001 | $675,000 |
| 2002 | $700,000 |
| 2003 | $700,000 |
| 2004 | $850,000 |
| 2005 | $950,000 |
| 2006 & thereafter | $1,000,000 |

Usually the state inheritance taxes also apply to the value of the estate at death. These laws vary from state to state, but frequently provide a credit for federal estate taxes paid and then assess a tax on the value of the estate minus the credit. Some states allow heirs to pay the inheritance tax in installments. Payment is always due at some fixed interval after the deceased person's death. Estate and inheritance taxes increase with the size of the estate.

## Documents of Estate Planning

The following are the important documents of your estate planning:

- ■ Your will (see the section "Drawing Up a Will" later in this chapter)

- ■ Your trust arrangements (if applicable)

- ■ Your estate inventory (see the section "Making an Inventory of Your Assets" later in this chapter)

- ■ Your documents regarding power of attorney, medical attorney, living will, and contact information for attorney, executor, guardian, and so on.

Place these documents in a safe place, perhaps a safety deposit box, and let your family or other significant people know where you keep these documents.

## Drawing Up a Will

The foundation for your estate planning is to have a *will*. This document comprises your written directions for the distribution of your estate after your death.

A will has several main paragraphs providing, among other things:

- **An instruction specifying the disposition of the deceased person's personal property.** This instruction is necessary because the law handles personal property (which includes such things as cash, stocks, bonds, collections, furniture, automobiles, and art) differently than real property.

- **An instruction making any specific bequests.**

- **Identification of the executor or executrix of the will.** This person supervises the collection and disposition of the assets, files the necessary court documents, submits the necessary tax returns, and insures payment of final debts. The difference between the executor or executrix and a court-appointed administrator is that *you* choose this person, not the court.

- **A statement of the specific actions that you authorize the executor to take on behalf of the estate.**

- **Instructions for distributing the remainder of the estate (everything that isn't personal property).**

Don't be taken in by the cheap and easy "do-it-yourself" will kits. An attorney should draft your will after extensive consultation with you. An attorney who is qualified to practice law in your state knows the laws of inheritance, the system of estate administration, and the proper language of the will.

## Making an Inventory of Your Assets

Your assets change over the course of your lifetime, but you should take an inventory now and update that list every year. Use the following form or modify it to suit your own special needs.

**An Inventory of Your Estate**

| *Assets* | *Account Number* | *Value* |
|---|---|---|
| **Cash in banks and money markets** | | |
| Checking | ———— | ———— |
| Savings | ———— | ———— |
| Money Market(s) | ———— | ———— |
| **Stocks (itemize)** | | |
| ———— | ———— | ———— |
| ———— | ———— | ———— |
| ———— | ———— | ———— |
| ———— | ———— | ———— |
| **Bonds (itemize)** | | |
| ———— | ———— | ———— |
| ———— | ———— | ———— |
| **Mutual Funds (itemize)** | | |
| ———— | ———— | ———— |
| ———— | ———— | ———— |

**Other Investments (Itemize)**

401(k)

_____                    _____                    _____

_____                    _____                    _____

IRA(s)

_____                    _____                    _____

_____                    _____                    _____

**Home, other real estate** _____                                   _____

**Car(s)**                                  _____          _____

**Personal property**              _____          _____

**Life insurance**                   _____          _____

**Business equipment, interest, and so on**          _____

_____

**Other (itemize)**

_____                    _____                    _____

_____                    _____                    _____

**TOTAL ASSETS**                                            _____

| *Liabilities* | *Source* | *Value* |
|---|---|---|
| **Mortgage(s)** | ———— | ———— |
| **Loans (itemize)** | | |
| ———— | ———— | ———— |
| | ———— | ———— |
| **Credit card debt(s) (itemize)** | | |
| ———— | ———— | ———— |
| ———— | ———— | ———— |
| **Taxes** | ———— | ———— |
| **Other** | | |
| ———— | ———— | ———— |
| ———— | ———— | ———— |

**TOTAL LIABILITIES** ————

**NET ESTATE (Subtract total liabilities from total assets)**

————

# CLIFFSNOTES REVIEW

Use this CliffsNotes Review to practice what you've learned in this book and to build your confidence in doing the job right the first time. After you work through the review questions and the fun and useful "Consider This" section, you're well on your way to achieving your goal of planning your retirement.

## Q&A

**1.** Why is retirement planning an important subject?

  **a.** The huge Baby Boom generation is approaching retirement age and has done a relatively poor job of saving assets for retirement.

  **b.** The stock market gains of the 1990s have provided many people with larger estates and a more expensive lifestyle than they may have anticipated.

  **c.** Society benefits when individuals provide for themselves after retirement, rather than becoming wards of the state.

  **d.** All of the above.

**2.** Beginning in 1998, if an employer-sponsored retirement plan doesn't cover you and you file a joint return:

  **a.** You may not deduct any of your contribution to a traditional IRA.

  **b.** You can deduct your entire contribution to a traditional IRA, even if an employer-sponsored retirement plan covers your spouse.

  **c.** You may be able to deduct all of your contributions to a traditional IRA, even if an employer-sponsored retirement plan covers your spouse. However, your deduction is limited to $2,000 and you must reduce the deduction further if the AGI stated on the joint return exceeds $150,000.

  **d.** None of the above

**3.** Defined benefit plans are:

   **a.** Qualified plans in which the employer decides whether to contribute on the employee's behalf.

   **b.** Qualified plans that completely favor highly paid employees.

   **c.** Qualified plans that assure that the employee receives a stated benefit at retirement.

   **d.** None of the above.

**4.** 401(k) plans are:

   **a.** Defined contribution vehicles that usually include a salary deferral and employee matching contribution.

   **b.** One of the most common qualified retirement plan types.

   **c.** Plans that may allow employees to invest in a number of different kinds of vehicles, including several different types of mutual funds.

   **d.** All of the above.

**Answers:** (1) d. (2) c. (3) c. (4) d.

## Practice Projects

**1.** Get a copy of the summary plan description (SPD) of your retirement plan from the human resources department of your employer. Read it, write down any questions you have on what you read, and then ask your HR representative those questions.

**2.** Order your Personal Earnings and Benefit Estimate Statement (PEBES) from the Social Security Administration. See Chapter 8 for the how-to.

## Consider This

■ Did you know that your employer is required to provide you with a summary plan description of your qualified retirement plan?

- Did you know that you can find out the amount of your vested benefit by looking at your annual individualized benefit statement (required by ERISA)?

- Did you know that if you participate in a 401(k) plan, you can probably adjust the amount of your salary that is deferred, direct your investments into an array of mutual funds, or take a loan from your account?

- Did you know that if you change employers, you can roll your vested benefit over into a rollover IRA? You can do this each time you change jobs, and you can use the same or a different IRA each time.

- Did you know that if you use a will, you can control the way your estate is administered and to whom your property is given after you die?

# CLIFFSNOTES RESOURCE CENTER

The learning doesn't need to stop here. CliffsNotes Resource Center shows you the best of the best — links to the best information in print and online about the subject of retirement planning. Look for these terrific resources at your favorite bookstore or local library and on the Internet. When you're online, make your first stop www.cliffsnotes.com, where we've put all kinds of pertinent information about planning your retirement.

## Books

This CliffsNotes book is one of many great books about retirement planning. If you want some great next-step books, check out these other publications:

**CliffsNotes Investing for the First Time,** by Tracey Longo, helps you to invest successfully the first time and to find the investments that are right for you. IDG Books Worldwide, Inc. ISBN 0-7645-8539-8. $8.99.

**CliffsNotes Investing in 401(k)s,** by Mercedes Bailey, offers valuable advice for the beginning 401(k) investor. IDG Books Worldwide, Inc. ISBN 0-7645-8544-4. $8.99.

**CliffsNotes Investing in IRAs,** by Mercedes Bailey, guides you though the process of finding IRAs that suit your needs and gives you tips on investing in them. IDG Books Worldwide, Inc. ISBN 0-7645-8545-2. $8.99.

**CliffsNotes Investing in Mutual Funds,** by Juliette Fairley, shows you how experienced investors evaluate funds and walks you through the process of picking a fund to match your goals. IDG Books Worldwide, Inc. ISBN 0-7645-8517-7. $8.99.

**CliffsNotes Investing in the Stock Market,** by C. Edward Gilpatric, gets you up to speed on stock market terminology while showing you how to build and update your stock portfolio as the market changes. IDG Books Worldwide, Inc. ISBN 0-7645-8518-5. $8.99.

**Investing For Dummies,** by Eric Tyson, shows you, in a step-by-step way, how to assess your financial situation, gauge risks and returns, and make sound, sensible investment choices. IDG Books Worldwide, Inc. ISBN 0-7645-5162-0. $19.99.

**Personal Finance For Dummies,** by Eric Tyson, cuts through the jargon and provides you with sound advice, expert tips, and recommendations for how to quickly get your financial picture in order. IDG Books Worldwide, Inc. ISBN 0-7645-5013-6. $19.99.

**How to Plan for a Secure Retirement,** by Barry Dickman, Trudy Lieberman, and Elias M. Zuckerman, with the Editors of Consumer Reports Books, gives lots of useful information, at a basic level in an easy-to-read format. The book includes an excellent appendix, with various worksheets, lists of state agencies, and lists of states that allow living wills or health care powers of attorney. Consumer Reports Books. ISBN 0-8904-3889-7. $29.95.

It's easy to find books published by IDG Books Worldwide, Inc., and other publishers. You'll find them in your favorite bookstores (on the Internet and at a store near you). We also have three web sites that you can use to read about all the books we publish:

- www.cliffsnotes.com
- www.dummies.com
- www.idgbooks.com

# The Internet

If you have access to the Internet, you can find an entire universe of helpful information on retirement planning. Virtually every fund manager, bank, and law firm that maintains a site offers something on the subject of retirement planning. Most likely, the owners of these sites hope to profit from your interest, either by providing services for a fee (lawyers and accountants, perhaps) or managing your retirement funds (brokerage firms and fund managers). Some of the most interesting sites that we've found are listed here. However, we urge you to conduct your own search because the sites change constantly.

**IRS — The Digital Daily, www.irs.gov,** offers tax forms and some excellent publications for download.

**Social Security Online, www.ssa.gov,** is the official site of the Social Security Administration.

**The Retirement Planning Center, www.belmontbank. com/retire_p.html,** gives good general information, provided by Belmont Bank.

**James Mallett's Retirement Planning Page, www.stetson. edu/~jmallett/retire.htm,** offers some good information on IRAs and Roth IRAs from Stetson University. The site includes Quicken's IRA Planner.

**Piper Jaffray's Retirement Planning Page, www.piperjaffray. com/si/si_rp.asp,** is an excellent site maintained by a major investment broker and advisor, and it includes a retirement calculator.

**Minnesota Mutual's Retirement Planning Page, www. minnesotamutual.com/solindiv/retire/retireso.html,** is an interesting site maintained by this fund operator. The material is aimed at older employees.

**4BabyBoomers, www.4babyboomers.com,** delivers just what the title says. The site includes a link to a retirement-planning section geared toward boomers.

**The DMBA Home Page, www.dmba.com/OLRetirement. htm,** lists a nice collection of links to other retirement sites.

Because of the dynamic nature of the Web, you should conduct your own Internet search. To help you search, you can use any or all of the following excellent search engines:

www.altavista.com

www.lycos.com

www.yahoo.com

www.askjeeves.com

# INDEX

# CliffsNotes™

**Your shortcut to**
# success™
**for over 40 years**

## Computers and Software

Confused by computers? Struggling with software? Let *CliffsNotes* get you up to speed on the fundamentals — quickly and easily. Titles include:

Balancing Your Checkbook with Quicken®
Buying Your First PC
Creating a Dynamite PowerPoint® 2000 Presentation
Making Windows® 98 Work for You
Setting up a Windows® 98 Home Network
Upgrading and Repairing Your PC
Using Your First PC
Using Your First iMac™
Writing Your First Computer Program

## The Internet

Intrigued by the Internet? Puzzled about life online? Let *CliffsNotes* show you how to get started with e-mail, Web surfing, and more. Titles include:

Buying and Selling on eBay®
Creating Web Pages with HTML
Creating Your First Web Page
Exploring the Internet with Yahoo!®
Finding a Job on the Web
Getting on the Internet
Going Online with AOL®
Shopping Online Safely